The Famine Years
In Northwest Donegal
1845 – 1850

By

PATRICK CAMPBELL

FIRST EDITION
Death in Templecrone
Copyright © 1995 by Patrick Campbell
All Rights Reserved

SECOND EDITION
Revised and expanded
THE FAMINE YEARS IN
NORTHWEST DONEGAL 1845 – 1850

ISBN 978-1515049104

Copyright 2015 by Patrick Campbell All Rights Reserved

Published by
P.H. Campbell
82 Bentley Avenue
Jersey City, NJ 07304
(201) 434-2432

BOOKS BY PATRICK CAMPBELL

A Molly Maguire Story (Revised Edition)

The Death of Franklin Gowen

The World Trade Center: The 1993 Attack: Unanswered Questions

Mad Dog Coll: And His Wife Lottie

The Famine Years In Northwest Donegal: 1845 – 1850

Napper Tandy & William Burton Conyngham: Lords of Burtonport

Memories of Dungloe, County Donegal: 1940 – 1960 (Revised Edition)

Ghosts?: Four Strange Stories

A Death in the Family: The Loss of a Child

Hurricane!!: The Night of the Big Wind: Donegal 1839

The Incident on the Pier Road: A Horror Story

Thanks to the National Archives, Dublin; the National Library, Dublin; the Donegal County Library, Letterkenny Co. Donegal; the Folklore Department, University College Dublin; AFRI, Dublin; and the New York Public Library.

Dedicated to the victims of the great hunger.

1800 – 1845	Rapid population increase. Food shortages. Adverse weather conditions.

Distress in Ireland in the 1840s: A Chronology, 1845 – 1850

1845	The partial failure of the potato crop.
1846	Total failure of the potato crop. A nation without the basic food of the poor tenant farmers.
1847	Widespread fever epidemics sweep over Ireland. Only half the normal potato crop grown. Evictions. Massive emigration begins.
1848	Potato crop fails again over most of Ireland. Fever epidemic continues. Evictions and emigration continue.
1849	Millions homeless. Economy destroyed. Fever epidemic worse than 1847.
1849	Irish continue to flee the country. The whole nation bankrupt. The potato crop is healthy.
1850	Distress continues, but the second good crop of potatoes in a row increases the food supply. The fever epidemic burns out. The Irish continue to pour out of the country.
1850 – 1880	Landlord tenant conflicts.

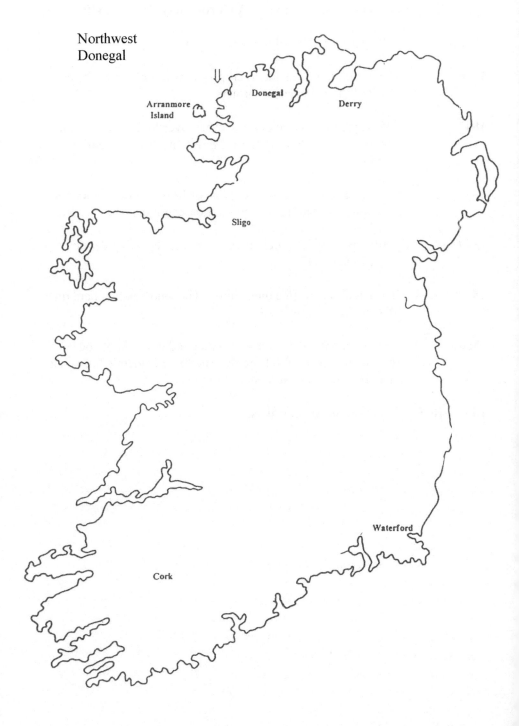

CONTENTS

INTRODUCTION
    Northwest Donegal: Before the Famine: 1800 – 1845   i
CHAPTER ONE
    The Famine Years in Templecrone Parish   1
CHAPTER TWO   4
CHAPTER THREE   9
CHAPTER FOUR   15
CHAPTER FIVE   24
CHAPTER SIX   33
CHAPTER SEVEN   39
CHAPTER EIGHT   55
CHAPTER NINE   67
CHAPTER TEN   80
CHAPTER ELEVEN   90
CHAPTER TWELVE   97
CHAPTER THIRTEEN   109
CHAPTER FOURTEEN   116
CHAPTER FIFTEEN   121
CHAPTER SIXTEEN   127
CHAPTER SEVENTEEN   133
CHAPER EIGHTEEN   138
CHAPTER NINETEEN
    Northwest Donegal: After the Famine   141
NOTES   156
BIBLIOGRAPHY   164

INTRODUCTION
Northwest Donegal: Before the Famine: 1800 – 1845

The failure of the potato crops in 1845 in Northwest Donegal was not the only reason that the residents suffered so grievously during the famine of the 1840s. There were a number of other reasons that contributed heavily to the casualties, including frequent storms that destroyed crops and drove fish out of the region; a rapidly increasing population; mismanagement of estates by the landlords who owned the land in the area; a tendency of tenants to focus on one crop—the potato; and the crowding together of increasing number of people into a limited number of farm holdings.

THE WEATHER

An analysis of the weather conditions during the early 19th century clearly shows that chronic rainstorms played havoc with the ability of tenant farmers to raise crops every year without the crops being destroyed by these storms. The gales that sprung up without warning sometimes took the lives of fishermen caught out at sea.

Chronic bad weather had battered the coastline of the Northwest for hundreds of years, and this weather pattern continued until the 1850s. This weather pattern was described by meteorologists as the Little Ice Age, which existed all over Europe from the 13th century to the mid-19th century. It was characterized by brutal winter and spring weather patterns, erratic cold and warm spells, and unpredictable squalls and hurricanes.

These adverse weather conditions made it difficult for tenant farmers to build up a reserve of food that would carry them over a bad year. As a result, many of these farmers were just one crop away from starvation and this set them up for a disaster when the crops failed several years in a row in the 1840s.

Brutal hurricanes did not just uproot crops, these storms also poured massive amounts of rainwater on the crops and soaked and damaged the soil. And those who were living close to the shore had crops destroyed by massive tidal waves that poured over the fields.

Many of the small farmers living along the coastline depended on the sea to supply them with the fish that was part of their basic diet. Shellfish and edible seaweed found along the shore were also an important part of their diet. But all of these foods were periodically destroyed by storms, which ripped the seaweed off the rocks and carried it out to sea, as well as destroying shellfish, which were tossed out on the shore and eaten by seagulls.

The weather caused major problems not only for the poverty-stricken tenants; it created problems for the landlords, because the tenants could not pay the rents. This in turn, created problems for the agents of the landlords, who were often dismissed for their failure to collect rents.

Some of the tenants who lived in the Rosses between 1800 and the 1840s grew weary of the never-ending struggle with the elements and the landlords and immigrated to America.

But it was only the more ambitious of the tenants who emigrated, and the majority remained on the land hoping that the endless cycle of storms would cease and they would be able to raise their families with some degree of security.

There were two reasons why people did not leave this hostile environment.

First of all, they viewed Northwest Donegal as their ancestral home, where their ancestors had lived in for countless generations, and they were attached to it, and were very reluctant to leave it and journey out into the unknown regions of the United States.

Another reason was the existence of the potato, which contained all the nutrients needed to sustain life, and enabled them to grow enough food on a half-acre of land to feed an entire family. Because of this most people who had small children were unwilling to abandon their homeland unless they were faced with the type of food shortages which threatened their very existence.

But the potato's positive features led to a dramatic increase in the population in the area, and this huge population increase was another of the causes of the catastrophe that was to take place in the 1840s.

There were a number of reasons for the increase in population.

First of all, parents decided to have large families because they believed these families were insurance for their old age: they wanted numerous young people around to take care of them when they no longer could take care of themselves.

The second reason was the decision of young people to marry at an early age, as young as sixteen, and they, in turn, had large families.

In 1760, the population of the Rosses area was 2,000 people living in modest cabins strung out along the coast and on the islands. A similar number lived in Gweedore, the parish to the north.

By 1800, the population in the Rosses had grown to 3,000, a 50% increase. In 1810, the population of the Rosses grew to 4,000 and to 6,000 in 1820. By 1830, it had increased to 8,000, and by 1840, there was 10,000 living in the area. It is estimated that by 1845, on the eve of the famine, the Rosses had a population of 12,000, six times the population of 1760. A similar dramatic increase in population occurred in Gweedore.

None of these population increases could be attributed to people moving into the area, because the Northwest offered settlers nothing but a basic existence based on a potato economy, and all the increases were the result of early marriages and a decision to have very large families.

The dramatic increase in population between 1800 and 1845 created a situation in which small farms of between five and ten acres were divided and subdivided among families until it reached the point where a single family who had lived comfortably on ten acres in 1800 was replaced by the families of their children and the families of grandchildren. The result was that as many as thirty or forty people were growing food on 10 acres instead of the eight or nine in a single family that had been farming the plot in 1800.

There were two byproducts of this subdivision of the land. First, the original lessee of the 10-acre farm may have improved his dwelling to include extra rooms and a slate roof, but the children of the original tenant who lived on the holding could only afford to build stone cottages with thatched roofs. The grandchildren, in turn, when given a plot of land could only afford to build a sod dwelling with a primitive roof. Thus, the standard of living was going down with each generation.

The second byproduct was that the original lessee used to diversify his crops: growing oats to make bread and porridge; wheat to pay the rent, and turnips to feed animals. All of these additional crops were a hedge against the hunger that could occur when a single crop, such as the potato, failed. As more and more subdivisions occurred, the diversification of crops dropped off and the result was a catastrophe when the potato crop failed.

Government officials who made surveys in the area in the 1830s and 1840s describe a landscape along the coast dotted with one-room thatched cottages with hordes of children running around outside, many of them half-naked. The adults wore ragged clothes and had faces blackened with smoke from the peat fires in the poorly ventilated huts. However, all the people, apart from the grime, seemed well fed, thanks to the potato.

John Donovan, the Irish scholar who was in the Rosses in 1835 conducting an ordinance survey, was horrified at the conditions he witnessed. He saw the ramshackle dwellings and total poverty of most of the people and he noted that the majority of the tenants had a dependence on the potato for food. It was Donovan's opinion that if the potato crop ever failed there would be a tragedy of catastrophic dimensions in the area. His prediction was accurate.

John Mitchel, the Irish political activist, passed through the Rosses in 1845 and was appalled at the condition of the tenants. He blamed Conyngham, the absentee landlord, but he did not seem to realize that it was the entire landlord system that was to blame, because he had favorable comments to make about Hill, the landlord in nearby Gweedore, whom he characterized as an improving landlord.

In reality, Hill was even more ruthless than Conyngham because he ruled his tenants like a tyrant and evicted anyone who displeased him.

Campbell Foster, a noted journalist with the *Times* of London, published an expose of the Conyngham estate in September 1845, on the eve of the famine, describing the overcrowding on Arranmore Island and the destitution of its people. He also put a public focus for the first time on the reason for the overcrowding: the subletting of small family farms into several even smaller patches.

The impression given by these visitors to the Northwest was that all the dwellings in the area were like those found in Africa, and that the people living there were as backward as the tribes of Africa.

The comparison to Africa was not quite accurate. The majority of the people in the Rosses did in fact live in conditions that were in many ways similar to the living conditions of natives of Africa. But those who surveyed the area neglected to note that there was a substantial minority of houses in the area that could be described as comfortable, with slate roofs, and there were also a considerable number that had multiple stories and were well furnished.

It was not noted either that the quality of housing and the standard of living had dropped from 1800 to 1845, all of which could be traced to several factors and not just to the policies of the landlords.

In 1800, 20% of dwellings that were listed in the census were described as either first class or second-class structures and were comfortable. These were mainly in the population centers of Dungloe, Burtonport, Rutland, and Arranmore. The first class houses had multiple stories and spacious rooms and were well furnished. The second class houses had slate roofs and had several rooms, and had furniture such as beds, tables and chairs, and even rugs on the floors.

Out in the countryside the standard of living dropped dramatically, however. Out there, the vast majority of the dwellings were one room cottages built with stone from the surrounding countryside. Very few of these cottages had furniture of any kind and the majority used straw thrown on the floor as bedding. As many as a dozen members of an extended family lived in these dwellings, which were classified by the census as third class dwellings.

There was a fourth class category and this made up 10% of the dwellings in the area in 1800. These were one room cabins, with walls built of sod, and roofs constructed of tree branches and rushes, with a fireplace usually in the center of the room. The smoke from the fire was allowed to ventilate through a hole in the roof. In these cabins, furniture was almost nonexistent. The occupants used the single room as a bedroom and a living room, and if the family were lucky enough to own a cow or a pig, this animal could often be found inside on a cold winter night.

The people who lived in the first- and second-class houses in 1800 were obviously more affluent than the 80% of the people who lived in substandard housing, and they were not as vulnerable as the poor of the area were to famine, because they had a varied diet and were not wholly dependent on the potato.

In the first three decades of the 19th century, the people who lived in the one-room cabins were well enough nourished by the potato diet, which was often supplemented by fish caught locally and by edible seaweed and shellfish gathered along the shore.

But the substandard dwellings were a very unhealthy environment for young children and there was a high death rate among the newborn in these damp, smoky cabins. Older people also died before their time because of the conditions within the cabins.

As the population rapidly increased in the years before the famine, and sub-grade dwellings accounted for 80% of the total number of dwellings, the majority of the population was reduced to destitution. A catastrophe was inevitable.

The extent of the destitution in Northwest Donegal on the eve of the famine is graphically illustrated by a report written in 1837 by Patrick McKye, a schoolteacher in Gweedore, the parish immediately north of the Rosses. The report was sent to the Lord Lieutenant in Dublin in order to solicit government aid for a community that was on the edge of destruction. Gweedore had a population of 9,000 at this time, and if McKye's report were accurate then the same conditions would have existed in the Rosses.

The following is a condensed version of the McKye report:

"To his Excellency the Lord Lieutenant:

The parish of Tullaghobegly [Gweedore] is in the neediest, most hungry, and ragged condition of any people that ever came within the precincts of my knowledge, although I have traveled a part of nine counties in Ireland, also a part of England and Scotland, together with parts of British America. I have also perambulated 2253 miles through some of the United States, and never witnessed the tenth part of such hunger, hardship, and nakedness.

Now, my Lord, if the causes which I now lay before your Excellency were not of very extraordinary importance, I would never presume that it should be laid before you. But I consider myself bound in duty to relieve distressed and hungry fellowmen, although I am sorry that my charity cannot extend further than to explain to the rich where hunger and hardship exist in almost the greatest degree that nature can endure, and which I will endeavor to explain in detail with all the truth and accuracy in my power:

There are about 9000 persons in this parish, and all are Catholics, and as poor as I shall describe, having among them no more than one cart, no wheel car, no coach, one plow, sixteen harrows, eight saddles, two pillions, eleven hurdles, twenty shovels, thirty two rakes, seventy table forks, ninety three chairs, two hundred and forty three stools, ten iron grapes, no swine, twenty seven geese, three turkeys, two feather beds, eight chaff beds, two stables, six cow houses, one national school, one priest, no resident gentleman, no bonnet, no clock, three watches, eight brass candlesticks, no looking glasses, no boots, no fruit trees, no turnips, no parsnips, no carrots, no clover.

None of their married or unmarried women can afford more than one shift change of clothes, and the fewest number cannot afford any, and more than half of both men and women cannot afford shoes, nor can many of them afford a second bed, but whole families of sons and daughters of mature age lying together with their parents."

This unhealthy standard of living increased each decade after 1800, and by 1845, it became the catastrophic situation witnessed by Donovan, Mitchel, and Foster.

When the potato failed the inhabitants of the third and fourth level housing were immediately put in harm's way by the shortage of basic food, and they were the ones who died first from hunger. But when outbreaks of cholera broke out in the area, the rich were as vulnerable as the poor, and many were swept away to their graves in the holocaust that followed.

One could argue that the potato alone was the cause of the disaster that followed the crop failures of the 1840: it was the potato that enabled families to exist on small patches of land; it was the potato that inspired young couples to marry; and it was the potato that enabled young couples to have large families, because the potato was able to feed these families.

But while there is no doubt that the potato was a major factor in the disaster, the landlord system of property ownership also played a major role, and had the population not been impoverished by high rents and small farms, they could have diversified crops and not been solely dependent on the potato.

The social organization of the Rosses was another factor that contributed to chaos that followed the crop failures. In the Rosses, a small minority of people at the top of a pyramid-type social structure reaped the benefits of the labor of the vast majority of people who occupied the lower rungs of society. All the affluence of those at the top flowed upwards from those at the bottom, and when the labor of the majority no longer created the wealth that sustained the minority, chaos followed.

The leading members of the social structure in the Rosses in the first decades of the 19th century were members of the Protestant community, who were descendants of the British settlers who conquered Donegal in the early 17th century. They made up only 7% of the population.

In order to be considered a member of the elite ruling class, one had to be a Protestant, a landlord, or a professional with a university degree, and have an important function in the parish.

The most influential members of the community were members of the Forster family, a resident landlord who owned less than 10% of the land in the area. The Forsters had been around for several generations and had served the Conynghams, major absentee landlords in the area, for many years as resident agent. Eventually the Forsters acquired enough land to become small independent landlords, and they in turn tried to get as much revenue out of their tenants as possible without driving them to destitution.

The Forsters lived in Burtonport and most of their tenants knew them personally. The family was ambitious and they made the most of the property they owned. Over the years, the Forsters had developed a kelp industry, which brought revenue into the area from sales of kelp to Scots and English buyers. This industry also benefited many of their tenants who gathered kelp along the shore.

The Church of Ireland rector was another prominent member of the community and was even more influential than members of the Forster family. The rector was usually the person who interacted with the authorities in Dublin when a crisis occurred locally, and he was the one who headed any local committee to deal with the crises.

During the famine, the Rev Valentine Pole Griffith, the rector for Templecrone parish, led the campaign to get food and medical supplies into the Rosses area, and he established soup kitchens in Dungloe and Maghery. He bombarded the government in Dublin with appeals for help almost on a daily basis, but his pleas were usually ignored, and if it were not for the help provided by a Quaker fact-finding mission in 1846, Templecrone Parish could have been decimated.

Prior to the famine, the Catholic population of the parish was resentful of the Protestant rectors because they were forced by the British government to support the Protestant church with 10% of their income. Later in the century, this tithing would be abolished.

The Forster family was also disliked by the Catholic population even though they created jobs in the area and were not characterized during the famine as abusive landlords. They were disliked because they were totally loyal to the British Crown.

When the Forsters were agents for Conyngham, Francis Forster, and his father before him, did their best to extract rents from impoverished tenants, but they resisted Conyngham's instructions to evict such tenants. One reason for this was that they knew evictions would be pointless because no other farmer would take over the land of an evicted family. A more important reason was that they lived among their tenants and depended on them for income, and even though there was little violence in the Rosses between 1800 and 1845, there was always the possibility that if a destitute family were evicted someone might decide to take revenge on the Forsters. So, they were always aware that they were a vulnerable minority.

The social elite in the area also included any doctor living in the area; the agent for the absentee landlord; top government officials like the head of the Revenue Police or the head of the Coast Guard; or any other professional person who was a Protestant. However, within the elite, there was a pecking order: those who belonged to the Church of Ireland considered themselves superior to Presbyterians, and Presbyterians considered themselves superior to Methodists or Baptists. All Protestants considered themselves vastly superior to Catholics—who they believed practiced the religion of rebels and heretics.

Members of this elite group socialized with one another; they sent their children to private schools; and they only married partners who had the same social standing as they had.

The second level of society was the owners of hotels, stores, or businesses of any kind. Some of these people were Protestant and some were Catholic, but none of them was considered "gentlemen" because they were "involved in trade"—an activity looked down upon by gentlemen. There was a great deal of resentment among the local businessmen at being treated as second-class citizens in their own home area.

The Boyle families and the Sweeney family of Dungloe and Burtonport were successful in business and yet they were not accepted as equals by the Forsters or the clergymen of the Church of Ireland.

These Catholic families believed they were direct descendants of the Boyle and Sweeney clan leaders who had ruled the Rosses before the area was overrun by the British several hundred years before, and they were not only proud of their own "aristocratic" heritage, they were inclined to look down on the Protestant elite whom they believed to have no claims to aristocracy at all.

The Protestant businessmen in the Rosses did not like been viewed as inferior by the elite either. The Hanlon Family in Dungloe and the Sproules of Burtonport had been relatively affluent for generations and they resented the fact that only landlords or professionals were seen as the elite of local society.

These Protestant businessmen also resented being lumped in the same class as the Catholic Sweeneys and Boyles, because they thought their Protestant heritage alone made them far superior to either family, and they believed their Anglo-Saxon genes entitled them to view with distain anyone who belonged to the conquered Celtic race.

When reporters from the *Times* of London visited the Rosses, they always referred to the Protestant rector, or members of the Forster family by name, but when they made a reference to the owners of the hotels, or the owners of other businesses in Dungloe or Burtonport, they never used a surname—they used a title: the inn keeper; or the store owner.

The Catholic clergy were not considered gentlemen either and they too were often referred to as the priests, or the Roman clergy. On occasion, in official reports, the name of the parish priest was used, but this was rare.

The next level down on the social order were the shop assistants, the hotel workers, the maids who worked in the more affluent homes, the subagents for the landlords, members of the Revenue Police, members of the Coast Guard, and anyone else who was earning a steady salary no matter how small it was.

These people could be very snobbish about their steady salaries and were inclined to look down their noses at anyone who earned a living at fishing or farming. It was their opinion that it took a certain amount of brains to be a white collar worker and it took no amount of brains at all to dig potatoes or catch fish.

The shop assistants in particular were very protective about their status in society. They were always well dressed during working hours and they were very much aware that they often dispensed credit to many of their customers who depended on this credit in order to survive. These shop assistants were inclined to patronize some of these customers.

Men and women in this social level were very careful who they married, and were fearful of marrying anyone of a lower social status.

The next level of society was occupied by the occupants of the stone cottages, who held the primary lease for the farms with the landlords. This group, and the group of subtenants they had on their property, were the workers who created all the wealth generated in the Northwest. It was these tenants who grew the wheat, oats and potatoes handed over to the landlords agents in lieu of rent; this group harvested the kelp that was turned into hard cash by the landlords and the storekeepers; this group caught the fish who were handed over to the landlords for salting, smoking and exporting; and it was this group who kept the storekeepers and landlords agents in business, because without their contribution there would be no wealth created in the Rosses or Gweedore.

And yet these residents of the Rosses received little respect from those who occupied rungs higher up on the social ladder, unless they managed to acquire enough assets to build slate cottages and rent larger farms, and in the process move higher up the social scale.

There were two separate lifestyles within the stone cottage community. There were those who lived on the islands and made fishing and the gathering of kelp their primary means of earning a living, and farming and raising cows and sheep a secondary occupation. Then, there were those who lived on the mainland and made their principle activity raising crops, cows, sheep, and pigs, with only a small minority engaged in fishing.

When the potato crop failed, those who lived on the islands and near the shore fell back on salted fish, shellfish, and edible seaweed as a supplement to their diet. Those who lived inland hunted rabbits and game birds and ate edible plants and weeds to supplement their diets.

The lowest members of Rosses society were those who occupied the sod huts that covered the landscape outside the main population centers. They lived in these huts with huge families and adults often appeared ragged or half-naked in public.

These subtenants were mainly the descendants of the family that owned the prime lease on the property, although the identity of which particular person was the legal leaseholder was not often very clear. If the male member of the family whose name was on the prime lease died his name still remained on the lease, although his son might now be the responsible male on the farm. Sometimes the same name remained on the lease for sixty years, even though the man who originally signed the lease had been dead for forty years. If the farm was large enough and had been subleased to descendants for or five different times, after several decades had passed there were first or second cousins occupying space on the holding, all of them planting potato seed on every available square foot of space.

Campbell Foster, the *Times* reporter who visited Arranmore Island on the eve of the Famine, blamed the absentee landlord for the incredible number of families crowding on to small patches of land. He stated that the landlord did not care how many people were on a farm as long as he got his rent.

In the 1800 census the sod huts were less than 10% of the housing stock; by 1846, 60% of the housing stock were sod huts and the parish was overrun with destitute people.

THE ECONOMY

Most of the economic transactions in the Northwest involved barter. Cash was handled or used by only a minority of the population. All of the small tenant farmers paid their rent in potatoes or grain.

The diet of the farmers was very simple and there was not a great deal that needed to be bartered from the storekeepers.

A typical daily diet for those who lived in the stone cottages in the countryside would usually be three meals of potatoes, supplemented by oaten bread or porridge, and occasionally a salt fish. Many of the tenants also poached trout and salmon from the lakes and rivers, although this was illegal.

A more affluent household would have had a barrel of salted fish sitting by the door, a bag of oats in a bin, and a pit near the dwelling that was full of a year's supply of potatoes. The inhabitants of the sod huts existed on a diet of potatoes alone, supplemented by some edible seaweed. Part of their potato crop was given to the owner of the primary lease as a contribution towards the rent of an acre or half acre. In order to acquire the means to buy clothing, tea, salt, or sugar, the children of these households were hired out to large farms in East Donegal for a six months period for a fixed salary. The male adults of these holdings went to Scotland to work on farms for the summer, or to work in Scottish ports gutting fish.

Somehow, the inhabitants of the sod huts survived and multiplied in an economy in which the potato was the cornerstone of the food chain, but when the potato failed the economy collapsed like a house of cards, and both the poverty-stricken and the affluent suffered an economic meltdown together.

The reasons for the collapse was obvious: the prosperity of the businessmen and their employees depended on the wealth generated by the poverty-stricken tenants, and the comfortable lifestyle of the landlords and their staff also depended on how much revenue they could squeeze out of small farmers who were at best only several months away from starvation.

With the loss of the potato crops the economy of the Rosses went into a free fall: the tenants had no food, or assets to pay the rent; the stores had no customers; and when the landlord was receiving no rent he terminated employees. The entire area became destitute.

A massive intervention by the Quakers and other charitable organizations prevented a horrendous loss of life, but when the famine era was over in 1850, thousands of tenants fled to the United States and never returned. And the population of the Northwest went into a deep decline.

CHAPTER ONE
The Famine Years in Templecrone Parish

In 1991, when I was involved in research in the National Archives in Dublin for a book entitled *A Molly Maguire Story*, I came across two reports written about conditions in Templecrone Parish, the Rosses, Northwest Donegal during the great hunger of the 1840s.

The first report described how hundreds of men, women and children crowded Main Street, Dungloe, the capital of the Rosses, in the winter of 1846, begging for food from a relief committee, which was meeting in Hanlon's Temperance Hotel.[1]

The second report described hunger and disease in Arranmore Island, in 1847 the island where my grandfather, Tim Gallagher, was born in 1855, and where scores of my cousins still live.

Both the scenes in Dungloe and Arranmore had been described by investigators sent into the area by the Quakers in December of 1846, and the reports had been published and widely circulated at the time.

I was surprised by these two reports because I had heard little about the famine when I was growing up in the Rosses, and even though my father and my grandfather had told me stories about the famine which they had heard from their parents and grandparents, these were stories of hard times and a scarcity of food, with only occasional references to fatalities—not the tales of horror involving a multitude of deaths that were portrayed in the Quaker reports.

The two Quaker reports intrigued me, but I did not pursue the subject at that time, as I was far more interested in the Molly Maguire research, and I continued to devote all my energy to that subject.

But the images created by the Quaker stories had made a deep impression on me and when *A Molly Maguire Story* was published in 1992, I decided to dig a little deeper into the history of the famine in the Rosses.

I had, of course, more than just a casual interest in the subject. I had ancestors on both sides of my family who were alive during the famine, and their experiences during this period were part of my family's history.

My decision to dig a little deeper into famine history coincided with a planned vacation trip to Donegal, and I decided that while I was there I would research the local folklore on the subject. My plan was to interview the oldest people in the parish, and also the people who had the reputation of being reservoirs of local history.

During the next two weeks I talked to scores of people about the famine and I got the same response from all of them: the Rosses suffered few casualties from hunger: it was believed that when the potato crops failed the inhabitants of the area turned to the seashore for food because the coastal areas of the parish had an abundance of fish and shellfish, and the people had managed to get by on those sources, which they supplemented with edible seaweed and weeds and cresses from the bogs.

Some said they had heard of a few deaths from famine fever, but the death toll from disease had not been high.

When I informed these people about the end-of-the-world scenes described by the Quakers, they argued that the Quaker reports must have been inaccurate or exaggerated because if there had been such widespread destitution they would have heard about it from their parents or their grandparents.

Nevertheless, as far as I was concerned the Quaker reports had the ring of truth to them, and in spite of the obvious conviction of those I had interviewed, I found it very difficult to believe that the Parish of Templecrone in the Rosses had few casualties and had survived the famine with very few deaths.

Since I had acquired no information on the famine during my two weeks in the Rosses, I decided I would go back to the source of the Quaker reports: the National Library in Dublin to see what else might be there that might help me resolve the obvious conflict between the Quaker view of the famine in Rosses, and the local view that the famine had left the parish unscathed.

The National Library, on Kildare Street, has an abundance of documents relating to all periods of Irish history, and the collections there are supplemented by other collections in the National Archives, Trinity College, University College Dublin, and in various other archives scattered throughout the city.

The first document I looked at were the census reports of 1841 and 1851. I selected these documents because I wanted to compare the 1841 census of the Rosses with the 1851 census, because I believed that there would be a dramatic drop in the population in 1851, which could be attributed to the famine years of 1845 – 1850.[2]

But an initial examination of the census seemed to indicate that Templecrone Parish lost only 250 people, a 2.5% decline from 9,842 to 9,592, which was far below the decline in some parishes in the West of Ireland which lost almost 60% of their population.

However, I had failed to take into account the natural increase in population in the Rosses between 1841 and the beginning of 1847, when fatalities began to occur in great numbers, and with this natural increase, the population in late 1846 would have been 11,300, and the decline, would have been 1,700.

This 15% rate of decline was still below most of the areas on the west coast of Ireland, but it was still a high casualty rate, and it indicated that the Rosses had not escaped the famine.[3]

During the next 18 months I visited Ireland on five different occasions, spending a great deal of time in Dublin, in the National Archives and the National Library, and during these visits I read scores of books written on various aspects of the famine. I read every issue of *The Londonderry Journal*, the weekly newspaper in circulation in Donegal and Derry during the famine. I read every issue of the *Times*, the London newspaper that provided immense coverage of Irish affairs, during the same period.

And I unearthed hundreds of letters, reports, testimonials, and miscellaneous documents all dealing with some aspect of the famine experience in the Rosses. I had never seen any of these documents published in any newspaper article or book before so it would seem that the information buried in these files had never been widely accessed before.

The portrait that emerged from these documents was that of a parish that was, in 1845, heading for a predictable catastrophe because of a rapidly rising population and inhabitants with a dependence on a single source of food -- the potato. It was a parish in which there was an absentee landlord who made no improvements and squeezed as much money as possible out of his tenants. It was a parish in which tenants had very few resources to fall back on if the potato crop failed.

But, the documents also revealed hidden strengths in the community that would help ward off a total catastrophe, and these strengths helped reduce the number of people who died from hunger, fever and stress-related fatalities.

However, even though the fatalities were fewer than other hard hit areas in Cork, Clare and Mayo, the death count was much higher than even I imagined when I began my investigation in 1992.

CHAPTER TWO

The British government had been aware of the destitution among the tenants of the Rosses for decades prior to 1845, but failed to do anything to assist the inhabitants of the area.

In the early 1830s and early 1840s, surveys had been conducted of the destitute areas of Ireland by George Nicholls, who had been sent on this mission by the British government. Nicholls filed reports about the extreme poverty of the residents of the Rosses and the failure of the absentee landlord, the Marquis of Conyngham, to do anything to assist them.[1]

The Conyngham family resided at Slane Castle, County Meath, and had owned most of the Rosses for centuries, but members of the family rarely visited this remote estate and showed no interest in the tenants.

The estate was administered by an agent who resided in England, and it was directly supervised by a subagent who resided in the Rosses. The agent visited the Rosses once a year; the 2nd Marquis of Conyngham, who owned the Rosses during the famine, had visited the area only once in his lifetime.

In 1835 the British government sent another investigator into the Rosses, Gaelic scholar John O'Donovan, whose assignment was to provide an English translation for each place name in the Rosses, and also to make a note of antiquities and major buildings in each area he visited. O'Donovan's work was part of an Ordinance Survey of Ireland, and O'Donovan traveled all over Ulster while working on the project.

O'Donovan arrived in the Rosses on October 13, 1835, and like most first time visitors to the area was amazed by the barren grandeur of the terrain, which is one vast stretch of bog land 15 miles long and eight miles wide, pockmarked with lakes and strewn with boulders which break the skin of the bog.[2]

After crossing the Gweebarra River at Lettermacaward, the rugged beauty of the Rosses emerges, with the Atlantic on the left pounding on the islands offshore, and on the right, towering mountains with names like Slieve Snaght, Crockator, Crovehy, Crocknasharragh, and Errigal, and in between the endless bogs which stretch as far as the eye can see.

There was no bridge across the Gweebarra River at this time and O'Donovan had to wait until low tide, when the sea had drained out of the Gweebarra estuary, to cross the river on a small boat. On the other side, he met a group of women who were carrying bundles of hand knitted sweaters and gloves as they walked to Glenties, a village further south, to sell their wares.

O'Donovan described the women as "comely," but he wrote that they were badly dressed and that their faces were blackened with peat smoke a condition he attributed to living in "windowless smoke filled sod cabins."

As he made his way north, through the Rosses to Templecrone Parish, he described the same bogs, hills, and boulders that I had known as a child, and as I read O'Donovan it was evident that very little has changed in the landscapes since 1835.

O'Donovan's observations about his visit to the Rosses are written in the form of letters, and are presented in scholarly prose, as if he was imparting great truths. The whole tone of the prose suggests that he was entering a remote territory that was alien to the rest of Ireland, and he comes across like a white American exploring newly discovered Indian Territory in the American West in the 1830s.

The first time that O'Donovan revealed his limitations was in his description of various people he met while on his way into the village of Dungloe. Meeting people with surnames common to the area, such as O'Donnell, Sweeney, Boyle and Doherty, he wrote the following about them:

"The ancient Irish families can be distinguished by their forms and features. The O'Donnells are corpulent and heavy with manly faces and aquiline noses. The O'Boyles are ruddy and stout, pictures of health when well fed. The O'Dohertys are stout and chieftain like, but have all good faces. The MacSweeneys are spirited and tall, but of pale color."

The above is, of course, absurd, because the surname of any given individual does not determine his or her physical characteristics.

Any person with a surname like Sweeney, could have a mother with a Boyle surname, and a grandmother whose maiden name was O'Donnell, and a great grandmother whose maiden name was O'Doherty. Thus, any individual in the Rosses would have the genes of all of the families in the area, and to state that people with specific surnames had distinct physical characteristics is engaging in fiction that would be ridiculed in this day and age.

But O'Donovan had readers believe that the Celts of Northwest Donegal were composed of tribes like the Indian tribes of the American West, and since many of these tribes, like the Sioux and the Apache, did have some distinct physical characteristics, he was able to convince his readers that the Irish "tribes" of Donegal, such as the O'Donnells and Sweeneys, were also unique breeds that could be distinguished from one another. In spite of his

Celtic heritage and his Catholic religion O'Donovan had little sympathy for these Gaelic-speaking Irish, nor did he identify with them.

As far as he was concerned the Gaels of this area did not speak the same Irish he spoke, and he viewed with disdain their pure Celtic blood, which he believed was unmixed with any other blood, because of the isolation of the Rosses. This was a negative factor as far as he was concerned. Indeed, he believed that if the people in this area had a transfusion of English blood they would be much better off, and it was the absence of this blood of the conquerors that made these Gaels an inferior people.

All of the above, of course, was written for the public record and became part of the documents compiled for the Ordinance Survey.

O'Donovan was one of those members of the Irish Catholic upper middle class of the period who believed that in order to be tolerated and accepted by the Anglo Irish establishment, they had to put distance between themselves and the vast majority of their fellow Irish Catholics, who were destitute and uneducated. And they believed that the more they abused their own people the more favorably the British and Protestant establishment would look on them.

The tragedy for the majority of Irish Catholics was that views such as those written by O'Donovan reinforced the deep seated prejudices of the foreign rulers of Ireland and made it easier for them to treat Irish Catholics as an inferior people.

When the great hunger struck, it also made it easier for the establishment to turn a blind eye to the devastation that swept across Ireland and to rationalize that this tragedy was not happening to ordinary people, but to the lowly, uncivilized barbarians who inhabited the bogs.

When O'Donovan was not abusing the Donegal Irish for the benefit of the British, he presents a great deal of hard data that is useful to the scholar who would like to get an idea of what life was like in this area in the 1830s.

His letters describe a completely isolated area, very heavily populated, with no services of any kind, and a population that was over dependent on the potato as a food source.

In a rare insight, he predicts that great tragedy will descend on Templecrone because of the dependence on the potato and he states that if there is a general failure of the potato crop it will be a major catastrophe for the residents of the area.

My reaction to the O'Donovan documents was, of course, negative. He described how his fellow Irish Catholics had been reduced to a condition that just bordered on being civilized, but he made no mention of how they got in this condition, or what options they had, if any, to improve their lives.

Above all, I resented his posturing, as if he were far superior to these uneducated serfs that he viewed with such disdain, because I believe that his options were equally limited because of his race and religion and one of the differences between him and the landless laborers of Donegal was that they knew they had been subjugated, and he, apparently, did not.

The O'Donovan attitude towards the Rosses was a prejudice I came across time and time again as I examined the material I had collected.

The voices that described the Rosses and its people often expressed contempt at the conditions they saw, and even those who were sympathetic to the plight of the impoverished people were patronizing. The majority of those who visited the parish and wrote about it were either Anglo Irish charity workers, government officials who were either Anglo Irish or British, or Protestant evangelists, and all of them looked down upon these destitute Irish speaking people.

The four local leaders who headed the relief efforts, the Reverend Valentine Griffith, pastor in the Church of Ireland; Francis Forster, a resident landlord; George Frazer Brady, the local doctor; and George Thompson, head of the British Customs in the Rosses were Protestants who were loyal citizens of the United Kingdom.

Even though they worked tirelessly to help feed the hungry, they believed they belonged to a separate race of people and this attitude was evident in their correspondence.

There were only a few documents which were written by the majority, and among those were Father McMenamin, the Dungloe parish priest; and Patrick Campbell and Cornelius Ward, two relief committee leaders who headed the Mullaghderg Relief Committee.

Father McMenamin was polite but demanding in his correspondence with the government relief agencies as he asked for help for his people; Campbell and Ward were outspoken and hostile towards Conyngham, the absentee landlord, and were polite but firm in their letters to the government.

But the correspondence of McMenamin, Campbell and Ward appeared only occasionally, and the vast majority of the other documents portrayed the Rosses and its people as the establishment saw it, and very little in these documents reveal how the victims saw this terrible tragedy unfold.

However, a hundred years later, in the 1940s, an independent Irish government sent representatives of the Folklore Commission to the Rosses to interview the oldest citizens, who were the children and the grandchildren of the famine survivors, and the 200 page collection, written in Gaelic, is the only real indication of how the "great hunger" was viewed by the Irish Catholics of the area.

As I read these accounts of the famine it became obvious to me that back in 1945, many people knew a great deal about what was going on in the Rosses in 1845 and could paint vivid portraits of the disease and death that swept over the parish.

The people who told the stories were the Seanachie—the story tellers—and the tragedy is that when those people passed on much of their knowledge died with them.

Only the physical evidence of the famine remains: the roads to nowhere which had been built by the Board of Works, and the great stone walls built in Termon, which were constructed just to give employment to the starving people.

The Reverend Valentine Griffith's rectory at Maghery is still there, and so is Conyngham's agent's house at Lackbeg. And the unmarked graves of famine victims, including some of my own ancestors, are in the bogs and hillsides all over the parish, the location of most of them long forgotten.

CHAPTER THREE

The ten thousand inhabitants of Templecrone Parish, the Rosses, in 1845 appeared desperately poor to a visitor. John O'Donovan noted the absence of a middle class or an aristocracy, and that there was only one small resident landlord, Francis Forster, of Roshine Lodge, near Burtonport.

According to the 1841 census of Templecrone, there were 9,842 people living in 1,718 dwellings. Dungloe, the capital of Templecrone, had a population of 449, living in 78 dwellings.

Sixty percent of the dwellings in Templecrone were sod cabins, built with rocks and peat and roofed with straw. Few had furniture, and heat was provided by a peat fire in the center of the cabin. Most of these cabins were without windows, and straw placed on the floor served as bedding.

Another 30% of the dwellings were one-room stone cottages with thatch roofs, and the inside of these cottages were as Spartan as those of the sod cabins. These cottages not only provided shelter for the family they also provided shelter for any animals the family might have had such as pigs, sheep or cattle.

There was a small minority of houses in the parish that had more than one room, and most of these were in Dungloe, along Main Street, and were the homes of those who were a little more affluent. These, too, were thatched, but inside they had some furnishings and were classified by the government as second class houses, as opposed to the third class stone cabins, and the sod huts which were in the fourth class.

The few houses classified as first class were owned by the local clergymen, the doctor, the chief constable, the more affluent storekeepers and the landlord's subagents and bailiffs. These houses were fully furnished and were comfortable. But the vast majority of the inhabitants of Templecrone had never been inside a first class house and could only dream about what it was like to live in such a place. For them, the smoke-filled hut was the only reality.

Visitors to Templecrone during the period were appalled at the living conditions of the majority of the people.[2]

The appearance of the people matched their living conditions: most were barefoot and all wore ragged clothes. The children were half naked. But contemporary observers also noted the physical beauty of the people and the friendly welcome they extended to strangers.

In spite of the living conditions, each of the primitive dwellings had numerous children playing around it, and as long as the potato did not fail these children had plenty to eat, and were reasonably healthy.

The potato was the only food consumed by most families. A pot of potatoes was boiled for breakfast; another pot for the midday meal; and still another pot for the evening meal.

The steaming pot of potatoes was emptied into a wicker basket and the whole family sat around the basket and helped themselves to the potatoes. Dogs, cats, and chickens who shared the home also got their share.

Ninety percent of the people of Templecrone did not have permanent jobs, because there were no factories in the area, nor were there any estates or farms that would have provided work. Those that did have jobs were policemen, clergymen, bailiffs, shop assistants and household help who worked in such stores as Boyle's of Dungloe, or in the inns owned by Johndy Sweeney and Patrick Hanlon of Dungloe.

All of the people who did not have permanent employment supported their families in a number of ways. First of all, the people rented two very important patches of land: one was used to grow the potatoes that were the basic source of food; the other was a strip of bog which yielded the peat necessary for heating the cold damp dwellings. Once a sufficient crop of potatoes had been harvested and stored in the pits and the peat had been brought home and stacked near the dwellings, a family had an abundant supply of food and heating for the rest of the year. This family might appear ragged and barely civilized, but the reality was that apart from their destitute appearance they had all the basics needed to sustain life: food, heat and shelter.

The amount of labor needed to cut and dry the peat and sow and harvest the potatoes took only six weeks, but this did not mean that the men, women and children sat back and relaxed for the other 46 weeks of the year. The landlord had to be paid his rent, the store owner had to be paid for groceries bought on credit; and then there was the necessity of acquiring clothing for the children.

The Templecrone economy was not a cash economy: most people did not have cash, and many did not even understand it. The Templecrone economy was based on barter, on credit, and on the exchange of labor for items of value. Only those at the top of the pecking order used cash—people such as the store owners, innkeepers, police and clergymen. All others were in some way involved in the barter system.

At the bottom of the social heap were the inhabitants of the sod huts, who had bartered potatoes or labor, or both, from a tenant in exchange for a half an acre of land and the right to cut enough peat for a year.

The tenant might have only five or six acres, but the tenant needed extra potatoes if the family was a big one, and so a section was rented to a landless family, who immediately threw up a shack using the materials that were abundant in the area: rocks, sand and huge blocks of peat. Scrap wood, heather and straw were used as roofing.

The inhabitants of the sod huts lived a precarious existence. Landlords disliked this idea of subletting property, but were unwilling to move against tenants, since often the subtenant was often a relative of the tenant and had nowhere else to go.

The landlord raised the rent of those who had subtenants but this did not stop the practice, since tenants sublet out of necessity, not because they wanted to.

The families who lived in the huts rarely had pigs or cattle, which were considered real assets, since cows could give birth to calves, which could be sold, and pigs could give birth to numerous offspring, which also could be sold. The tenants who had such assets, however, used them to help pay the rent.

The subtenants and the tenants without livestock became involved in many activities in order to survive.

One of the ways the rent was paid was for the sub-tenant to work for up to a month for the tenant and also to have his whole family involved in harvesting the tenant's peat. This enabled the tenant to devote more time to his crop of oats or barley which was often given to the landlord in lieu of rent, or to devote more time to his cattle and pigs.

Those at the bottom of the social heap also sent their children out to work at the age of 10 for rich farmers in East Donegal and Tyrone, where they worked 14 hours a day, six days a week for six month periods, sleeping in barns and existing on bread, potatoes and water. The money these children earned helped pay the grocer's bills and buy some needed clothing.

The children left Templecrone in groups, walking over the mountains to Letterkenny, where they lined up for inspection on Market Square and were selected by the farmers on the basis of their strength and their ability to do the lowest type of farm work. The children were unsupervised by adults from Templecrone and were like slaves for the period they were in the employment of the farmers.

Adults also left Templecrone for seasonal work to make ends meet. Married men and single men and women went in groups to work in the potato farms of the Scottish lowlands.

It was not just the residents of Templecrone's one-room cottages who left the area for seasonal work all those who had no means of support, regardless of their living accommodations also headed out to get rent money, because if they did not, their families starved or they were evicted.

The women who remained at home had a number of ways of generating income, including raising chickens and selling them to the inns, or keeping the chickens and selling their eggs to Johndy Sweeney of Dungloe, a wholesaler who in turn shipped the eggs out to stores in Letterkenny and Derry.

In exchange for the eggs, the women got tea, sugar, salt and other commodities. Cash was rarely a part of the transaction.

Most women in the area were involved in knitting socks, gloves, and sweaters which they sold to wholesalers, and again they used the proceeds to supplement the family income.

All this activity—the work of the women and men, both at home and in Scotland, did not elevate families out of extreme poverty. Most families had so many young children that all resources were used in raising them and in paying the rent, and at the best of times the vast majority of the people of Templecrone were living from month to month, with the cornerstone of their entire economic system the lowly nutritious potato which insured the basic supply of food and all the nourishment needed to sustain life.

* * *

The residents of Templecrone who lived on the coast, or on the islands, had slightly different economic systems from those who lived up in the hills or back in the bogs. The potato was also the critical food in those areas, but an important supplement were the fish they were able to catch and the shellfish they gathered along the shore. Seaweed was an important part of their diet and was a substitute for potatoes in times of shortage.

The coast dwellers and islanders also sold fish to supplement their income and those who could catch enough fish during the year did not have to go off to work in Scotland.

Gathering seaweed for use as a fertilizer was another source of income, because this seaweed, spread over the potato fields was often the only fertilizer used by the poor, and it was traded by the people living along Templecrone's coast to those who lived inland, for potatoes, oats or other food.

Kelp was gathered and processed for export, and whole families along the shore were involved in this industry, providing them with enough income to enable them to pay the landlord.

Winkles, mussels, cockles and other shellfish were gathered for consumption by those who were short of potatoes, but most people in the area stayed away from this type of food because it was viewed as the food of the destitute.

But the fishing industry as such could not support the people of Templecrone because there were too few people involved in it and those who were did not have the gear or the bigger boats to fish in the rough seas of the open Atlantic. Most fishermen had very small boats, suitable for fishing in inlets, and not at all suited to venturing far out to sea where the greatest concentration of fish was. Even for these fishermen, the potato remained a critical element in their diet.

During one period, in the late 18th century, when there were huge shoals of herring, mackerel and cod off the coast, the Conyngham family invested heavily in fish processing facilities at Inis Mhic an Doirn, an island between Arranmore and Ailt an Chorrain. The family built a village and several factories on Inis Mhic an Doirn and renamed the island Rutland in honor of the Duke of Rutland who helped the family get government financial aid for the project, and they built more facilities at Ailt an Chorrain on the mainland and renamed it Burtonport, in honor of a branch of the family named Burton.

The Conynghams had visions of creating a vast fishing empire in the North Atlantic, with Rutland and Burtonport as the headquarters. Then, the shoals of fish vanished, and the Conynghams were left with all those state of the art facilities that were being used far below their capacity for decades afterwards. From that point onwards, the Conynghams lost interest in Templecrone and rarely visited it, being content to milk the tenants with high rents, and never again tried to make improvements on their estate.

But even if the Conynghams had been successful with their plans to launch a major fishing industry, it would not have been a great boon for local fishermen, who still would not have had the boats or nets for deep sea fishing. The Conyngham plans would have only benefited the big investors in the fishing industry—those who owned trawlers—and the local people at best would have had jobs gutting fish, or cleaning up on the big trawlers when they were in port.

However, even this would have brought some money into the area and given some employment, and had the industry thrived, the effects of the famine in Templecrone fifty years later would not have been so extreme.

When the famine did strike, the small boats at first gathered enough fish to feed many families, but the fishermen could not both feed their families and also sell enough fish to pay their rents, and as the famine progressed the boats and the gear were sold to satisfy the landlord's rent and the fishermen starved like the rest of the people.

CHAPTER FOUR

The political and social system in place in Great Britain and Ireland in the 1840s played a major role in setting the stage for the Irish famine.

Both political parties in the United Kingdom were controlled by aristocrats who were major landlords and these leaders had a vested interest in maintaining the landlord system.

Those who owned great estates, especially those with great estates that had been in the family for centuries, were venerated in Britain by all levels of society, and even the more liberal newspapers referred to the great landlords as "lords of the soil" or "esteemed noblemen."

This reverence was granted to these aristocrats because of their titles and amount of property they had inherited, not because they had achieved anything in life on their own merits.

Most Irish landlords had absolute control over their lands and "lords of the soil" was an appropriate title since they could do as they pleased with their tenants, including evict them if they wished.

The majority of the English landlords lived on their estates and there evolved in Great Britain a relatively good relationship between landlord and tenant, as landlords found it more productive to treat tenants fairly, and the tenants in turn worked hard to improve their farms knowing they would not be evicted. But both tenants and landlords in England knew who the master was.

The majority of Irish landlords did not live on their estates but lived either in the Dublin area or in London, and some never visited their Irish estates, while others, like the Marquis of Conyngham, visited them only once in a lifetime.

Many Irish landlords viewed their estates as mere investments that were milked to support a lavish lifestyle, and these landlords put agents in charge who resided on the estates and who made sure every penny of rent was collected.

Over the centuries, Irish estates became increasingly mismanaged as revenues were taken out and no improvements made. While English based landlords helped improve their estates and encouraged tenants to be more productive, estates like the Conyngham estate increased rents if improvements were made and this discouraged tenants from making any improvements.[1]

Criticism of Irish landlords in Britain was directed at them for their failure to manage these assets, not for mistreating their tenants. The British media and the British aristocracy granted men like Conyngham the "sacred right" to do as they pleased with their estates, but when swarms of destitute Irish laborers began to flee these estates and arrive in British cities, where many of them wound up on public assistance, then the British power structure saw the mismanagement by the Anglo Irish landlords as a threat to Britain's economic wellbeing.

The first Conyngham had come to Donegal from Scotland as a clergyman and settled in Mounthcarles in 1621. Each successive generation of the family became more affluent, marrying into the best families and inheriting estates and titles along the way. The family acquired the 40,000 acre Templecrone estate in the 17th century, and while it was a questionable investment at first, it was paying handsome dividends by the end of the 18th century.

The Conynghams lived in one of Ireland's great country homes, Slane Castle, and it remains today one of the finest privately owned residences in Ireland, and is in the possession of Lord Mountcharles, a direct descendant of the 2nd Marquis of Conyngham.

The Conynghams were social climbers from the very beginning. When George IV of England visited Slane 1821 as a guest of the Conynghams, the family had climbed to the top of British society.

During this visit to Slane, the King fell in love with Lady Conyngham and made her his mistress, with her husband's permission, and the King showered both of them with gifts: she received antique furnishings and expensive jewelry; he received many titles, including Baron Minister of Minister Abbey, Kent; General Officer in the army; Constable of Windsor Castle and Lord Stewart of the Household 1821–1830.[3]

The English titles, Constable of Windsor Castle and Lord Stewart of the Household, were the King's way of insuring that the Marquis would spend a great deal of time in the royal presence, and this, in turn, would insure that his wife would be available to grace the King's bed.

This intimate relationship with the royal family gave the Conynghams great power and put them beyond the reach of any British government who might have problems with the way they ran their estates. The 1st Marquis died on December 28, 1832 and he was survived by Elizabeth, his wife, who lived for another 30 years, and enjoyed immense prestige because of her relationship with the King.

The second Marquis of Conyngham, Francis Nathaniel, who inherited all the estates in 1832, was 24 years old when his mother became mistress to the King, and he, too, was showered with titles, even while little more than a boy. He was named Member of Parliament for Donegal at 24; Under

Secretary of State for Foreign Affairs at 26; Lord of the Treasury at 30; and Lord Chamberlain at 38. While in his 20s, he was also a general in the army and a vice admiral of the province of Ulster.[4]

Contemporary writers indicate that the Marquis had no qualifications for any of these titles, and the only experience that could be remotely related to any of his titles was his love of yachting which had some relationship to the title of vice admiral of Ulster.

It was obvious, therefore, that the younger Conyngham had leapfrogged to the top, not because of his talents, but because his mother was mistress of the King.

This inner circle influence would be a great asset to him in the 1840s, when he was being accused of being responsible for the deaths of hundreds of his tenants in Templecrone. These accusations might have brought down a less influential family, but the Conynghams were by this time immune from punishment.

Of course, the Conynghams were not the only Irish landlords who were immune from retribution for what happened during the famine. Scores of other aristocrats were also immune, because in the final analysis, the British aristocracy was not going to punish a fellow landlord, no matter how many of his tenants died in Ireland.

Although some of the inhabitants of Templecrone may have been aware that a new potato disease had attacked the crops in the European continent during the summer of 1845, it is doubtful that the news created much unease in the area.

The majority of the tenants in the area perceived a greater threat in the relationship they had with Conyngham whom they viewed as a tyrant. They were particularly hostile to Robert Russell, Conyngham's subagent, whom they considered vicious.

Two weeks before the blight made its appearance near Dublin, some of Conyngham's tenants were given an opportunity to fight back against their master, and they took advantage of the opportunity.

A journalist from the *Times*, of London, named Thomas Campbell Foster came to Templecrone to interview Conyngham's tenants about conditions in the area, and some of the tenants vented their anger at Conyngham to him. The article on Templecrone was published in the *Times* on September 3, 1845.

The article was an all-out attack on Conyngham and his agents, who were portrayed as tyrants whose only interest was to get as much money as possible out of the tenants, without giving anything in return. In the same article, Lord George Hill, a landlord in neighboring Gweedore, was portrayed as the model for enlightened Irish landlords, who ran his estate profitably but who also encouraged his tenants to improve their holdings.[5]

The *Times* was the most influential newspaper in the English-speaking world at the time, and this article must have hit the Marquis like a thunderbolt and humiliated him before his peers in the House of Lords.

However, there obviously had to be a great deal more to this article than just an example of crusading journalism that was designed to bring justice to the beleaguered tenants of Templecrone. Traditionally, the *Times* focused on subjects that impacted on the stability of the British Empire and a lengthy article on the poorest parish in one of the poorest counties of Ireland would not have made any particular sense unless the *Times* had another agenda.

Two possible reasons for the *Times* article were: the article was part of the *Times* long-running attack on Irish landlords who were blamed for all of Ireland's destitution; a personal vendetta against a Whig landlord by a Tory newspaper which disliked both Whigs and Irish landlords, especially Conyngham, whose close relationship with the Royal Family had made him immune to attack until his patron, George IV, died in 1837.

The attack on Conyngham is interesting for a number of reasons. Supposedly it was written to put the spotlight on the plight of the tenants, but the whole tone of the article patronizes the tenants and characterizes them as dirty, unsophisticated, immature and ignorant people who needed an enlightened Anglo-Irish landlord like Lord George Hill to guide them to a better life. A second article, published in the *Times* on September 16, this one exclusively on Hill, described Hill's tenants in the same patronizing way, and Hill is offered up as an example of a "good" landlord who could take worthless people and turn them into productive laborers who lived in comfortable homes.

Reading between the lines, it was obvious that the *Times* was on a crusade to change the way estates were managed in Ireland and they were prepared to do battle with Conyngham in order to draw attention to their crusade. It was convenient for the *Times* to have Hill in possession of an adjacent estate, because it enabled the newspaper to present an argument that badly managed estates produced destitution, while well-managed estates produced happy peasants living in neat well-kept cottages.

However, the attack on Conyngham was more than just a segment in a campaign against absentee landlords: the very way that the information was gathered and the venom with which it was written smacked of a personal vendetta.

When the *Times* decided to write the article on Templecrone, neither Conyngham nor his chief agent Benbow or his subagent Russell were contacted for information, or for clarification of charges made against them in the article. No effort at all was made to give them their day in court.

Instead, Campbell Foster contacted Francis Forster, the small resident landlord in Templecrone, and asked him to be his guide as he interviewed tenants in Dungloe and Arranmore.

Francis Forster had been Conyngham's local agent until 1833, when he had been dismissed and his job given to Russell. Forster hated Conyngham and Russell, his agent, and saw to it that the *Times* journalist saw the most destitute of Conyngham's tenants, who lived in Arranmore, and heard their story. When he was escorting the journalist to Arranmore Island, he deliberately walked him past Russell's residence at Lackbeg, to take a boat from a pier near the Russell residence.

Forster is presented in the article as a landlord who, when he agent of Hill had helped turn the Gweedore estate into such a well-run property and Forster's character is contrasted favorably with that of Russell, who was portrayed as presiding over the chaos of Templecrone.

There are a number of problems with the *Times* article, some of which are obvious; some of which are not.

First of all, the Conynghams had been the focal point of unfavorable reports before, in 1830 and 1832, when the British government sent investigators into Donegal to investigate the status of tenants in the area. Francis Forster and his father presided as agents over Conyngham's tenants at that time. Indeed the family had been Conyngham's agents for fifty years before that so Francis Forster had been the same kind of agent in the 1820s and 1830s that Russell was in the 1840s, and because of this he had little moral right to criticize Russell. The *Times* journalist was aware of Forster's past relationship with Conyngham, and so he knew he was using a biased source for his information.

The biggest problem with the article is that it was advocating a new way of managing Irish estates without revealing the full implications of the changes it was advocating.

The whole thrust of the article was to condemn the Rundale system in place in Templecrone, in which farms were sublet and subdivided to the point that a tenant might have a five-acre holding that was scattered in 20 different patches; each a quarter acre or less. This patch-quilt tenancy had come about through the subdivision of holding as fathers gave children a piece of the property, or inherited a strip of communal land that had been divided up among all tenants.

Since most tenants were "tenants at will" and could be evicted by the landlord, Hill, in Gweedore, had taken advantage of his power to evict tenants in order to end the Rundale system by forcing the tenants to abandon all holdings, and he then divided up the estate into units of five or ten acres and offered these units to some of the old tenants at greatly increased rents.

Those who accepted his offer had to build their own cottages and work twice as hard just to pay the rent, and most of them were little better off than they were before. Those who did not accept the offer, and there were many, had their homes demolished and they were evicted from the estate. Many found shelter in primitive shacks along the roadside, and many died of exposure in these shacks.

Hill, however, made almost three times the income of his predecessor, and did so while keeping vast tracts of his estate off limits to his tenants—tracts that they had used by the tenants as common ground for grazing their cattle or sheep. He also restricted use of the shoreline, which the tenants had used to harvest kelp.[6]

With his profits, Hill built a huge company store at Bunbeg, Gweedore, in which his tenants were forced to shop, and he monopolized the export of gloves, scarves and shirts knitted by the women on his estate which was another source of revenue to him. He also built a hotel on the Clady River, using cheap labor from his tenants and feeding his guests with produce bought at bargain prices from his laborers.

Hill's tenants who survived the reorganization of the estate were little better than slaves who were devoid of any rights. They could do nothing without the landlord's permission: they could not build a barn; build a fence; fish in the river or along the shoreline; or sell their holding to someone else. They were, in fact, the property of the landlord, and the only difference between them and the hundreds who were dumped on the roadside by Hill was that they were owned by Hill and the evicted were without a master.

Campbell Foster did not mention any of this, but instead contrasted the "well run" estate to the condition of the Conyngham estate. No word at all about the agony of eviction, or the humiliation of living like slaves.

Indeed, Campbell Foster was advocating that Conyngham should treat his tenants the way Hill had, and evict them all from their hovels; square off all the lots into neat well defined farms; and then let a limited number of them back on the property at twice or three times the rent, so the landlord could make enough money to make improvements, like a company store or a company hotel.

The problem with this plan, logical though it may be for the landlord, was the effect it had on the tenants who were evicted. Where would they go? How would they get enough food to feed their families? Would they be allowed to die on the roadside?

None of the above is dealt with in the *Times* article, even though the effects of such a reorganization should have been very obvious to the editors of the *Times*.

Of course, the real solution to destitution was one that was eventually imposed on the Conynghams several generations after the famine: the British government bought the land from Conyngham and sold it at a low price to his tenants. When the tenants owned their own holdings, they developed them, and destitution gradually vanished from the parish.

* * *

The *Times* article cut Conyngham to the bone and he decided to fight back or have his representatives fight back. Gentlemen like Conyngham never engaged in combat themselves, they always had others do the fighting for them.

Conyngham's agent, Benbow, a British MP, sent a letter to the *Times* in late September with a response written by Robert Russell, addressing the many accusations made in the Campbell Foster articles. The following is Benbow's cover letter.[7]

"Sir:

To The Editor of the *Times*

Having been absent in some remote parts of the country, I had not the opportunity of seeing your commissioner's report relative to the estates of the Marquis of Conyngham in Donegal, and your strictures thereon, till the 20th instant.

After perusing, I transmitted them to Mr. Robert Russell, a magistrate for the county of Donegal, and his lordship's local agent, and desired that he should immediately furnish me with a reply to them.

Adverse as I am to public discussion of a personal nature, yet in justice to Mr. Russell, and indeed to all parties, and more especially to an amiable and highly honorable nobleman who is a kind and considerate landlord, I feel myself bound to send you Mr. Russell's letter, and to request that you will be so obliging as to insert this letter in your next publication.

> I am, sir, your most obedient humble servant,
> John Benbow
> Crogenhouse, Corwen, North Wales, September 30, 1845"

Russell's reply to the charges leveled against him and his landlord was vigorous: he claimed that far from being an evil landlord, his lordship was a benign and generous ruler who tolerated rents long overdue and who never evicted anyone unless they absolutely refused to pay any rent.

Russell claimed that Conyngham had made numerous improvements to his property and did not pass the cost of these improvements on to his tenants.

Then Russell took a swipe at Francis Forster; he stated that there had been many problems with the estate when he took it over in 1833. He said the estate had been mismanaged by the previous agent and he was still cleaning up the situation he had inherited.

Finally, he criticized the *Times* reporter for failing to visit him while in Templecrone, stating that he even walked right past his door and took a boat to Arranmore from the pier next to his house. He claimed Campbell Foster had been very unfair to Conyngham and could have got the true story had he only seen fit to visit the agent while he was in Templecrone.

If Russell thought he had successfully fought back against the *Times*, he was badly mistaken, because Campbell Foster, who was in Tuam, Co Galway, when the Russell article was published, wrote a furious rebuttal that was even more critical than the first broadside. He began his rebuttal by referring to Russell's past career as a domestic servant and then went on to say that he was a liar who was getting his master into even more trouble.

He took every one of Russell's arguments and pointed out the errors in them, and quoted from previous government surveys of Templecrone to argue that Conyngham had made no improvements and had raised his tenants' rents if the tenants made improvements themselves.[8]

Campbell Foster's second diatribe was more damaging than the first broadside in September, and obviously Conyngham, Benbow and Russell had made a critical error in provoking the *Times* reporter. They would have been much better off had they ignored the first article entirely.

The majority of the tenants of Templecrone could neither read nor write, so they were unable to read the ping-pong of charges that were going back and forth in the pages of the *Times*. But there were those among them who could read and these people translated the substance of the debate into Irish and this in turn was told to the people around the turf fires in the sod cabins, and the tenants were amazed that such lofty individuals should wage war over their brutal existence in the remote glens of Donegal.

There were some who believed that good would come of this that Conyngham would be forced to treat them with more humanity, but nothing could have been further from the truth. A month later when one third of the potato crop was wiped out and help was needed for the hungry of Templecrone, Russell said Conyngham would give no help, and Russell stated that the tenants could eat rotten potatoes, which were good enough for them.

It was obvious that Conyngham and Russell believed that the tenants were part of the plot to disgrace them and the tenants would pay a price for this in the years ahead.

CHAPTER FIVE

In June of 1845, the British newspapers reported that a new blight was decimating potato crops on the European continent. This blight was capable of not only wiping out whole crops in stricken areas, but also of moving rapidly from one area to another.[1]

As the cause of the blight was unknown, there were as many opinions about what caused it as there were scientists.

The potato crop had failed frequently in Europe before, but there were never total failures, and the failures had many origins, including the weather. This particular failure, however, struck fear in the hearts of farmers, because it struck so suddenly, was so devastating, and moved from one area to the next with the speed of lightning.

The blight was first spotted in Dublin on September 16, and it spread rapidly through the country in the next eight weeks. The only redeeming feature of the 1845 blight was that it arrived late in the season, after the first crop had been harvested. Potatoes were often planted in two crops in Ireland, the first one in April or May, and harvesting of the crop began in July and August. A second crop was set in May or June and was harvested in September and October.

Both crops were stored in pits dug in the fields and it was from these stores that the small tenant farmer and his family drew their food supply for the year.

When the blight first became widespread the first crop had already been harvested and a great deal of it had also been consumed. Some of the second crop had still to be dug and it was this crop that suffered the initial attack of the blight.

The blight that devastated the Irish potato crop was a fungus that had originated in America and traveled across the Atlantic in an infected potato in the hold of a ship.

The nature of the fungus was unknown to scientists in 1845, and it was not until 1860 that it was identified as a minute fringelike growth that is composed of long slender branching filaments. The tip of the filament has a capsule of spores.

When the spore containers mature, some drift off in the wind while others fall and make their way down to the potatoes in the ground. The spores attack the potato leaves and the potatoes in the ground with incredible vigor. The entire plant above ground can be reduced to a blackened hulk overnight, and the potatoes in the ground, including those stored in pits, can be reduced to mush during the same period.[2]

Known as phytophthora infestans, the blight can only thrive in and multiply in the right weather conditions.

The right weather conditions are damp muggy days with a light breeze blowing. The blight needs drops of water to germinate and a gentle breeze to blow the spores across the landscape. A periodic drizzle is ideal; a pouring rain is not suitable at all. High winds destroy the spore. The weather in Ireland in 1845 had just the right combination of elements for the blight to prosper and multiply.

When the blight struck, Prime Minister Peel appointed a scientific commission which was ordered to study the blight and find ways of combating it. Since these scientists did not know the cause of the disease or how it multiplied, any solution they came up with was at best an educated guess.

Peel's scientific commission suggested that the peasants line potato pits with lime and store the potatoes there, but this proved useless. The commission suggested that if the diseased potatoes were baked at 180 degrees Fahrenheit they would turn white. They did not. And it suggested that potatoes be grated and mixed with oatmeal to make pancakes, but the result was not only disgusting, it made those who tried it sick.

The cause of the blight was thought by many to be static electricity generated in the clouds by the puffs of smoke from the locomotives which were coming into use. Others thought that droppings from seagulls caused the disease. Still others blamed the devil. Nobody knew the real cause.[3]

In Templecrone, with its rich blend of Catholicism and Celtic superstition, everything from the wee folk to airborne magic from Africa were thought to have caused the blight.

People gathered in the fields and prayed for the potato crop to survive the winter of 1845, and then blessed the fields with a rabbit foot for good luck. Some were afraid to go out at night in case it was the devil who was ruining the crops because they were afraid they would meet him doing his evil work.

Educated men all over Ireland and England made bizarre suggestions about how to cope with the disaster, but all suggestions came to nothing, because the potatoes that had been infected were destroyed and nothing at all would bring them back to life again.

However, the blight of 1845 did not devastate all of the crops or all of those stored in pits: the disease skipped over fields and even whole areas and only one third to one half of the entire crop had been destroyed.

The blight struck Templecrone on October 13th and one third of the crop was wiped out.[4]

In spite of the blight that was threatening the potato crops there was no premonition in Donegal of the disaster that lay ahead.

On October 2nd, Lord George Hill threw a large reception for his tenants on his Gweedore estate and gave out scores of cash awards for the best crop of potatoes; the tidiest garden; the best kept cottage; the best fences. All of Hill's tenants were required to be on hand, and so were agent Forster and sub-agents Chambers, Ramsey and Law.[5]

All the Protestant clergy were present and so were local Protestant businessmen, such as Charles Sproule of nearby Burtonport, and Sir James Stewart of Dunfanaghy.

The *Londonderry Journal* heaped lavish praise on Hill as the ideal landlord who ran a successful estate without abusing his tenants.

Given the tone of the article in the *Londonderry Journal*, it was very evident that Hill appeared to be ruling his fiefdom in Gweedore like an absolute monarch, and that every other "gentleman" in the area deferred to him.

One hundred miles across Ulster, two weeks later, an even bigger and more lavish reception was given by the Marquis of Hereford for 7,000 of his tenants at Lisburn, County Armagh.[6]

This worthy nobleman had to hire 300 waiters to serve the food to his assembled subjects, and the fare that was served was fit for a king.

According to the *Londonderry Journal* the banquet featured 70 sides of roast beef; 55 sides of roasted mutton; 97 joints of boiled beef; 92 hams; 95 tongues; 192 meat pies; 72 turkeys, 72 geese, and 3,600 pounds of bread. These were washed down with 3,200 bottles of punch, 30 barrels of beer, a keg of ale a keg of porter, and a cask of cider.

The tenants who were guests came from 200 townlands in the Lisburn area and collectively they paid the landlord 70,000 pounds a year in rent—about $17 million in today's currency. This esteemed lord of the soil had this revenue pouring into his bank account every year, and he had done nothing to earn it.

Although he had owned the estate for years, Hereford, like Conyngham, was an absentee landlord, and this was the first time he had visited his source of revenue, so he decided to mark the event by throwing a party.

But then, given his income from the estate, he could well afford it.

In Templecrone, Conyngham's tenants, who had never seen a side of roast beef, never mind partake of it, would not have believed that such a landlord as Hereford existed. But, as far as the awards given by Hill were concerned, most of Conyngham's tenants believed that the Gweedore tenants paid for these awards one way or another.

In a way, the Templecrone tenants could accept the cold mercenary attitude of Conyngham, which was far less offensive than the patronizing attitude of both Hill and Hereford, which really demeaned the tenants.

By the end of November in 1845, the full extent of the potato failure in Templecrone became apparent and plans were formed in order to combat the food shortage.

The failure of one third of the second crop was viewed as a serious problem but not as a total catastrophe. There had been food shortages in previous years and they had been coped with through government aid, charity, and community self-help.

The difference between this potato failure and previous potato failures was that this time the culprit was not bad weather, late frost, or potato diseases that the people were familiar with, but an unknown assailant that had destroyed crops overnight.

The first line of defense for the people of Templecrone was the Gaelic customs, which called for sharing in time of crisis. People not only helped out distant cousins in an extended family, but custom called for helping out anyone who came to their door looking for aid, no matter how limited the resources of the host. It was considered a taboo to turn away someone from one's door who needed food or shelter.

The folklore on the famine gathered in 1945 by the Folklore Commission is full of stories of neighbors helping each other out with food in the autumn of 1845. Each family in the area had a pride in their ability to be self-supporting, but each family knew they belonged to a community that supported each other in times of crisis.

The way this assistance was given in Templecrone was a reflection of the deep rooted pride each member of the community had, no matter how humble their circumstances.[7]

Gifts of food were often left at the door of needy families during the night, with the giver knocking on the door to alert those inside, and the giver then quickly disappearing into the darkness.

Thus those who received the food did not suffer the embarrassment of having to accept charity in person from a neighbor, and the givers did not have to suffer the embarrassment of "lording" it over those less fortunate than themselves.

In late 1845 there was a great deal of giving and receiving in Templecrone because of the way the blight had struck the area.

The blight had swept across the area in a checkerboard fashion, striking one small farm and skipping over the next two farms. Thus a tenant who lost all his potatoes might have neighbors on each side of him who had a healthy crop, and the neighbors with potatoes would allot a portion of their harvest to keep hunger from the door of a stricken neighbor. The vast majority of the families shared with each other in 1845 and 1846, and those that did not were viewed with contempt.

This Gaelic code in normal times extended beyond the sharing of food. If illness struck the man of the house and left him incapacitated, neighbors would plant his potato crop, harvest them, and keep an eye on his livestock, and on his family.

If a man died, and he left a big family, help would either be given to the widow, or neighbors would take some of the children and raise them. If the mother in the household died, and there were small children in the family, the father was expected to marry as soon as possible in order to provide the children with a mother. All of this reaching out to one another in time of crisis was one of the great strengths of the residents of Templecrone, and this self-help saved many lives during the famine years.

Writers like Campbell Foster or even the Quaker investigators might not have been aware of the sophisticated and indeed very civilized social network among the people of the bogs and mountains of Northwest Donegal. These visitors only saw the diet, the sod cabins, the illiteracy, and the Gaelic language, and they came to the conclusion that these people lived on the fringes of civilization.

The reality was that behind the destitution was a warm and caring network of relationships that was far superior to the uncaring materialism of the big cities of Ireland or Britain, or the brutal individualism that was typical of the British and Anglo-Irish aristocracy.

In early November, after the initial shock of the potato failure, the leaders of the Templecrone community got together to draw up plans for dealing with the widespread food shortages which were inevitable in the months ahead.

Even an early crop of potatoes would not be available until the following June, and in the meantime the parish had lost a large percentage of its crop of potatoes, and somehow funds would have to be raised in order to buy food so that the more destitute families in the parish did not starve.

There were five leaders of the relief effort in Templecrone, all of whom occupied positions of power in the community.

One was the Reverend Valentine P. Griffith, Officiating Minister, Church of Ireland; then there was the Reverend McMenamin, the Catholic Parish Priest; a third was George Frazer Brady, the Medical Superintendent for the area; then there was R. Thompson, Inspecting Officer of the Coast Guard; and finally there was Francis Forster, Justice of the Peace, agent for Lord George Hill, and landlord in his own right.

These five men were in fact the elite of Templecrone society. There was a sixth influential person in Templecrone Robert Russell, Conyngham's agent, but he would not join the Relief Committee nor would he participate in any type of relief effort, no matter what it involved.

Each of these five men on the Relief Committee had emerged as a local leader because of his position in local society. Griffith and McMenamin were clergymen, and as clergymen they had prestige and power second to none in the community. Brady was the leading doctor in the area and he enjoyed immense prestige because of this. Forster was a judge, a landowner, and a relatively wealthy man, and he, too, had a high standing in the community.

And Thompson, of the Coast Guard, was a government representative and he had the power that went with being a senior government official.

There were others in Templecrone who had a high social position, like Johndy Sweeney of Sweeney's Hotel, Dungloe, who was a Catholic; and the Hanlon family who owned Hanlon's Hotel, Dungloe, who were Protestant. But neither Johndy Sweeney nor Patrick Hanlon were invited to join the committee because they were not "gentlemen" of the caliber of the other five, and would, therefore, never be considered by the establishment as leaders of their community.

In reading the contemporary newspaper accounts of the progress of the famine in Templecrone, and also the accounts of the Quaker investigators who came to the area, it is interesting to note how class conscious all of these visitors were. In writing about Johndy Sweeney of Sweeney's Hotel or Patrick Hanlon of Hanlon's Hotel, these men were never referred to by name always as "the innkeeper."

The only persons in Templecrone who were referred to by name in these accounts were the "gentlemen": Forster, Griffith, Brady and Thompson. The parish priest, Father McMenamin, was not considered a "real" gentleman either, because he is only described as the Roman priest or the parish priest. Of the five men on the Committee there were two natural leaders: the Reverend Valentine Pole Griffith, and Francis Forster. Both Griffith and Forster were very effective at fund raising and they immediately began to send out urgent appeals for help once the extent of the pending food shortages became evident.

Griffith had extensive contacts in the Church of Ireland hierarchy and he used his influence to send urgent appeals to a network of friends all over Ireland, asking that collections be taken up for the people of Templecrone. Forster, too, had many contacts in Dublin and Belfast and he visited both cities to describe the conditions in Templecrone and the need to send food there as soon as possible. It is probable that some of Forster's dedication to helping the destitute was motivated by compassion, but it must be noted that he had also financial reasons for his involvement in this activity. Forster had hundreds of tenants who were living on the edge of starvation at the best of times, and they had to devote a great deal of their resources just to be able to pay the rent to him.

Forster had, like Hill, consolidated his holdings when he bought them and turned them into small farms rented out at a high rent –farms which produced oats, barley, turnips and cabbage, in addition to potatoes. In addition, his tenants also raised cattle, pigs and chickens. But potatoes were still the main diet of these tenants, with the other crops and livestock mainly sold to pay the higher rent, and any extensive potato failure would force these small farmers to eat oats and eggs instead of selling them, and this in turn put Forster's rent at risk, and this was another reason why he worked so hard to get free food delivered to the parish.

A second reason was that his more affluent tenants would be forced by custom to share their food with those who had no food at all, and this again put his rents even further at risk. Finally, it was the policy of the British government to make local taxpayers pay for relief given to the destitute, either as a hand out or as wages in public works projects, and in order to avoid having to pay huge bills for famine relief, Forster had an incentive to get as much aid as possible in the form of charitable contributions. So, he became a dedicated fund raiser, motivated by self-defense, so that the destitution of his tenants did not also send him to the poorhouse.

The Reverend Valentine Griffith would seem to have had an economic reason too for fund raising: he had 600 acres rented to scores of tenants, and it was the income from these rents which supported the Protestant church. But judging from his correspondence and his activities during the famine, it is very obvious that Griffith was only interested in the welfare of the people of Templecrone, both Catholic and Protestant, and economics played little or no part in his tireless efforts to feed the hungry.

* * *

As the extent of the potato failure became evident in Templecrone, Conyngham's agent moved quickly to secure the rents that were due at the end of the year, moving rapidly across the 40,000 acre estate demanding early payment in late October instead of late December. Russell knew that he was in fact taking all the food that these tenants had, leaving them with no food to feed their children, but he was not concerned by this. Those who lost their potatoes gave up their oats and barley in order to insure at least shelter for the coming year, and those who had neither barley nor wheat, but had young cattle or pigs handed over these animals. Thus, Russell was assured that his master would have the rent, even if his tenants died of hunger.

The small farmers who sublet sections of land to landless laborers in exchange for a portion of their crops were put in special jeopardy when the potato crop of the laborers failed. Not only did they not get the percentage of the laborer's crop, they were forced to pay Conyngham the rent on the laborer's land.

November and December of 1845 was a time of stress and deprivation for many of the poorer families of the parish.

There were 500 families out of the 1,700 in the parish who were made destitute by the potato failure and these families confronted starvation in the early months of the food shortages.[8]

Even though they were hopelessly poor, these people had a great deal of pride and the idea of being forced to beg for food cut them to the bone.

Many of the destitute had severe physical problems by December, because they would not ask for help for either themselves or their families, and they relied entirely on the generosity of friends and neighbors, but even this type of help was galling to them.

Some of these families got food on credit from local merchants, but these merchants could not give credit to everybody, and they were forced to refuse some requests.

While the food supply in Templecrone shrunk in the immediate aftermath of the failure of the potato crop, oats, wheat, and maize became available in local stores for those who could afford to buy them.

The demand for these grains, which had been imported from outside Templecrone, quickly drove up the price of these commodities, as those who had surplus assets bought up these foods as substitutes for the destroyed potatoes.[9]

Potatoes were also available, but at twice or three times the price during the summer, and again the forces of supply and demand were at work.

However, the destitute laborers who had no surplus assets to buy oats or barley had no means of acquiring the available food at any price, and their only hope was to either get work in order to get money to buy food, or get the food free.

Meanwhile, Russell, who with the help of his bailiffs, had gone around the parish gathering up all the grain and livestock as rent payments, had the grain processed in the huge Conyngham grain mills in Dungloe and then shipped to the Conyngham granary in Burtonport.

As his tenants grew more destitute Conyngham exported shipload after shipload of grain and livestock out of Burtonport, while his tenants watched, seething with anger along the shoreline.

Forster also shipped much of his grain and livestock out of Burtonport for sale abroad; however, he sold some to those tenants who could pay cash, and he also supplied local merchants who could afford to pay him.

He gave none of it away, however, and he devoted all his energy to getting charitable people in Dublin, Belfast and London to pay for the food which would keep his tenants alive.

CHAPTER SIX

When the blight was first reported in the European media, the news was monitored closely by the leaders of the British government, who hoped that this new blight would not find its way into Britain and Ireland.

British Prime Minister Robert Peel was worried, and so was Irish Catholic leader Daniel O'Connell, and both were worried for the same reason: a failure of the entire potato crop would be a major disaster for Ireland, given the Irish dependence on the potato. For remote isolated areas in the west, like Mayo and Donegal, a total failure could be worse than a disaster, it could be a catastrophe.

Peel and O'Connell had different concerns over the potato failure. Peel, whose nickname was "Orange Peel," disliked the Catholic Irish and cared nothing for their welfare, but he was worried that a major famine in Ireland could be expensive for British taxpayers and also could lead to major civil unrest in Ireland.

O'Connell on the other hand was worried about his people's survival and afraid the British would not come to their rescue if conditions got out of hand. He had good reason to worry, given Britain's track record in Ireland.

When the blight made its first appearance in Ireland on a farm outside Dublin on September 16, 1845, the worst fears of both Peel and O'Connell were realized, and both were forceful in seeking remedies that would protect their respective constituencies.

Sir James Graham, the Home Secretary, asked Peel for help for Ireland on October 13th and Peel responded by stating that he would try to get the legislation known as the Corn Laws repealed.

The Corn Laws were laws which protected British farmers from competition from abroad, by imposing huge tariffs on imported grain, and by restricting direct imports of grain to Ireland.

Peel wanted the Corn Laws repealed for two reasons. First, he wanted Irish landlords to be responsible for taking care of their own destitute tenants, and the importing of inexpensive American corn would be an incentive for the landlords to begin relief efforts. Peel viewed Irish destitution as an Irish problem and even though he insisted on British political and military control over the Irish people, he rejected any British responsibility for feeding Ireland's hungry at the expense of the British taxpayer in the event of a famine.[1]

Peel also wanted the Corn Laws repealed for an entirely different reason. Peel believed that there should be no government meddling in private enterprise, because he was a believer in the concept that businessmen had every right to engage in free trade, and that this was good for the businessmen and good for the country. Indeed, he not only believed that businessmen be allowed to conduct business as they pleased without restriction, but that landlords should be given the same freedom, namely that they could evict tenants or raise rents without interference.

The Corn Laws were viewed by Peel as an impediment to private enterprise and as an evil that kept the price of food artificially high, and he was determined to abolish them, even though the British landowners who gained by these laws had a powerful lobby in Parliament.

Daniel O'Connell was also opposed to the Corn Laws, because they benefited only British farmers and prevented Irish farmers from selling their grain wherever they pleased. Irish grain importers were also hurt because they had to buy grain through British wholesalers and have it shipped through British ports.

So, O'Connell had no quarrel with Peel's initiative in repealing the Corn Laws, because he believed it would benefit Ireland.

However, O'Connell knew much more than this would have to be done if a calamity was to be avoided: he believed that only intervention on the part of the British government would provide a way of avoiding a major disaster.

O'Connell called a meeting with the Lord Mayor of Dublin, John L. Arabin, and other concerned Irish leaders on October 28th, in Dublin's City Assembly House, and during the meeting O'Connell outlined what he and the other leaders believed ought to be done.

First of all he believed that all distilling and brewing be banned in Ireland immediately as this consumed vast quantities of grain that could be put to better use in feeding the multitudes who would need food in the coming year.

Next, he proposed that the export of all food should be prohibited immediately, and this included grain, vegetables, livestock, butter, eggs, fish, and all the other foodstuffs exported to Britain for British consumers. Also, he demanded that Irish ports be allowed to receive food directly from foreign countries.

Then, he wanted the government to intervene in the marketplace directly by buying provisions and making them available to the destitute Irish people. O'Connell pointed out that the government gained £74,000 a year the equivalent of $15 million in today's currency from taxes on the Irish export of wood, and that the British were using that money to beautify Windsor Palace and Trafalgar Square. Let this Irish money be used instead to head off famine, he argued.

O'Connell wanted all resident landlords taxed 10% and absentee landlords, like Conyngham of Templecrone, taxed 50%, and the revenue used for famine relief.

Finally, he wanted to begin public works projects immediately, like building a national railroad, so the destitute could earn enough money to buy food, and he asked that relief committees be formed in each county, so that a mechanism was in place to cope with the disaster he saw careening down towards his people.

O'Connell led a delegation to meet Lord Heytesbury, the Lord Lieutenant of Ireland, at his mansion in Phoenix Park. They were received with icy correctness by his lordship, who disliked intensely the idea that this delegation should presume to offer advice to his government on how to conduct its policies.

O'Connell had a high level delegation with him, but this did not impress his lordship. Among the 30 delegates were the Duke of Leinster, the Lord Mayor, John Augustus O'Neill, Sir James Murray, Henry Grattan and Lord Cloncurry.

O'Connell presented his proposals and Lord Heytesbury listened frostily to the presentation and when he had finished, Heytesbury said he would pass the proposals on to the government, and after that he ushered them out the door, with undue haste, given the high level of the delegation. Next day all Dublin was talking about this cavalier treatment, which was interpreted as telling the delegation that the British government was unconcerned with famine problems. "Let them starve," was the message to the Irish.

* * *

Peel's next move to combat rapidly deteriorating conditions in Ireland was to appoint a relief commission, which would come up with a plan to deal with the famine. The Relief Commission had its first meeting on November 20, 1845.

On the Relief Commission was Sir James Dombrain, Inspector General of the Coast Guard Service; Colonel Harry Jones, Chairman of the Board of Works; J. Twisleton, the Poor Law Commissioner; Colonel McGregor, Inspector General of the Constabulary; John Pitt Kennedy, the Secretary of the Commission; Edward Lucas, Chairman of the Commission; Professor Robert Thane, the only Catholic in the group; and Sir Randolph Routh, who was in fact in charge of the relief effort under the direction of Charles Edward Trevelyan, the head of the Treasury Department, who approved all projects.[3]

Two of these men would have an extremely negative impact on relief efforts in Templecrone: one was Charles Edward Trevelyan, who disliked the Irish and only gave help when it was too late; the other was Routh, whose initial "R" is all over the correspondence relating to relief efforts in Templecrone.

Peel's plan to combat the famine did not involve giving away free food to the starving Irish, even if they were dying.

He believed that if the Irish were given free food that they would never try to earn the money to buy it, and that the result would be that the British taxpayers would be burdened with feeding the Irish year after year.

So, distributing free food was out of the question and other ways had to be devised which would get food into the hands of those who needed it without interfering with the financial wellbeing of Britain.

Peel's attitude was, of course, rooted in his conviction that it was not the function of government to become involved in social programs but rather to insure that the rights of landowners and businessmen be protected. However, he was also a firm believer that Britain had to be protected from the poverty-stricken Irish masses, and he was determined that the Irish taxpayers pay for Irish poverty, and he would see to that even if this hurt the business interests of Irish landowners, most of whom lived in Britain and were, like the Marquis of Conyngham, powerful members of the British establishment.

It was an indication of the evolution of the British political system at that time that an appointed politician like Peel would consider instituting policies that were a threat to the financial wellbeing of the aristocracy. A hundred years prior to that the monarch would have had Peel beheaded for being presumptuous. Peel's plan for famine relief had a number of elements. First, he mandated the setting up of relief committees which would raise the taxes in each locality and this, in turn, would finance relief efforts in each area.

Then, under pressure to provide some government aid, he agreed to loan the Irish Board of Works the finances needed to set up public works projects in all hard hit areas, and this would give employment to the destitute.

In certain instances, some of the financial aid was given as a grant, but most of the financial aid was given as a loan, and every area was legally bound to repay this money once the area got back on its feet.

Finally, he dealt with the problem of assisting those who were not only destitute but homeless, by authorizing the setting up of additional poorhouses and fever hospitals, but again these facilities were to be constructed mainly with loans not handouts, and the bill would eventually come back to haunt the areas that had benefited.

The Peel plan for dealing with the famine was totally inadequate for dealing with the situation in Templecrone. The plan might have worked if the parish had a huge tax base of wealthy estates, or if there were many industries located in the area that could bear the financial burden of feeding the hungry and guaranteeing that the loans for public works would be repaid.

But in this wild mountain area of bogs, lakes and endless rows of boulders, there were no factories, no huge resident landlords and no middle class, and therefore the Peel plans were a recipe for disaster.

The Prime Minister did, however, recognize that there were places such as Templecrone where the supply system might be "inadequate," so on his own initiative, he purchased £100,000 of American maize, which he had distributed to depots in the west, including one of Conyngham's warehouses in Burtonport. However, these supplies were only extreme emergency supplies which were to be sold to the people at market prices and only if the supply of food available from local merchants dried up and food was unavailable.

Peel, and his representatives, Trevelyn and Routh, did not under any circumstances want the government to go into business in competition with local merchants, so the stores had to be empty and the people totally destitute before the corn could be sold, but even then it would only be made available to those who could pay for it.

Obviously, this regulation while it might have benefited the few who had some money, provided no benefit to the majority of the people who had no food, no job, and no means of earning money, and since these were the most vulnerable of all, the effect of these regulations was to place a great many people in Templecrone at great risk of losing their lives.

As 1845 came to a close, and demands increased all across Ireland for assistance to combat food shortages, many of the Tory newspapers published stories that claimed that conditions in Ireland were not nearly as bad as the Irish claimed.

The Evening Mail stated that the exaggerated claims of destitution being made were part of a plot to swindle the English, and the *Times* claimed that the Irish as usual wanted something for nothing.

Lord Heytesbury published a statement on November the 20th that demanded that all Irish landlords should call a meeting on their estates and determine what was needed and draw up plans to deal with shortages.

Conyngham's agent announced on November 27th that he was not calling a meeting and that his lordship was not interested in drawing up any plans, and if others were to draw up plans he would not participate in any program proposed. The agent stated that his lordship was not interested in relief committees, proposals for public works that would make him financially liable, or in generating work on his estates for the tenants.

Peel's attempt to get the Corn Laws repealed did not pass a House of Commons vote and he resigned on December 5th, and Lord John Russell, the Liberal leader, was invited by the Queen on December 8th to form a cabinet. But on December 25th he was back in Buckingham Palace to tell the Queen he was not able to form a government, and the Queen informed Peel he must continue as Prime Minister.

Peel went before the House of Commons and told the assembly that Ireland was faced with a major famine and that if the Commons ignored it, England could pay a heavy price. Again he argued for the repeal of the Corn Laws. But there was a great deal of hostility to Ireland in the Commons and few English members were in any mood to help Ireland out even if her destitution threatened England.

In Templecrone, on December 13th, Francis Forster wrote to his friend Sir James Stewart in Gweedore that he was apprehensive that the tenants in the parish would have no seed potatoes for the 1846 crop, because they would be forced to eat the seed to survive. Forster said the tenants should purchase oats and eat the oats instead of the potato seed thus saving the potatoes.

But he made no mention in the letter about how the tenants were going to get the money to buy the oats.

CHAPTER SEVEN

As the inhabitants of Templecrone endured hunger and brutally cold and wet weather in January and February of 1846, Francis Forster and the Reverend Valentine Griffith continued to beg for aid in both Britain and Ireland, and they used the funds they raised to buy food for the more destitute families in the parish.

In late February, another new relief committee, The Mullaghderg Committee, was formed in the parish, led by Cornelius Ward and Patrick Campbell. There were numerous townlands represented on this committee: Arlands, Cloghglass, Glennahilt, Meenagowna, Lackenagh, Acres, and Milltown.

The members of the committee who signed a petition to the Lord Lieutenant had Catholic names: Condy Boyle, John Gallagher, Daniel Ward, Owen Gallagher, Anthony Ward, Manus Ward, Neal Ward, John Coll, Anthony O'Donnell, Daniel Boyle, John Boyle, John O'Donnell, Bryan Ward, and Michael O'Donnell.[1]

The petition was dated March 27, 1846, and it dealt with issues critical to the people of the parish.

According to the committee there were 500 families in the parish who had only five weeks of provisions left, and another 200 families had no provisions at all and were totally dependent on others for food. There was a total of 1,700 households in Templecrone during this period, so obviously a large percentage of the population was already in trouble. The committee stated its opinion of Robert Russell, Conyngham's agent:

"Your petitioners further beg leave to inform your Excellency that they place no confidence whatsoever in Mr. Russell, Marquis of Conyngham's agent, for this reason: that applications are being made to him on the impending famine, and the redress given to the applicants that rotten potatoes was good enough for them—excellent encouragement at the approach of a famine. Your petitioners are of the firm belief he would feel a good deal of pleasure in seeing said tenants in extreme want inasmuch as that he charges some of these persons with being instrumental to the *Times* correspondent being brought here."

The petitioners then asked the Lord Lieutenant to see to it that employment was created for the destitute poor, so that they could earn the money needed to buy food for their families.

The formation of the committee was an interesting development for a number of reasons. First of all there were no "gentlemen" among them, and none among them either who had become leaders because they had wealth or huge farms.

Patrick Campbell had a house and two acres of land in Keadue; Cornelius Ward, who was also from Keadue, had a house and an acre and a half. All the other committee members had similar small holdings.[2]

The absence of a priest among the petitioners was unusual, since the Roman Catholic clergy at the time viewed themselves as leaders of the Catholic community.

But the most unusual aspect of all of this committee was that it dared to be openly critical of the very landlord who owned their homes and small farms and who had the power to evict all of them if he wanted to.

Their courage was not rewarded, however, the Lord Lieutenant sent the letter off to Routh and Routh took no action on it and filed it away.

Robert Russell, no doubt, added all those tenants who had signed the petition to his list of people who he would like to see suffer in the impending famine. However, Cornelius Ward was not about to let his friends and neighbors starve without further effort, and on April 11th, he wrote to Captain Kennedy, who headed the relief committee in Northwest Donegal, requesting that that shipments of meal be sent to Burtonport that could be sold at market prices.[3]

Ward's concern was that scarcity of meal and potatoes was driving up the prices in local stores, and that if meal was made available in ample supply by either the government or private relief agencies, then the price of food would be affordable to those who had money.

Ward also informed Kennedy that there were 500 able bodied men in Templecrone waiting for jobs on public works but that there was no hope that public works would be initiated by Conyngham and that he personally had no faith in Russell. So, could Kennedy help out in any way?

Ward's communication to Kennedy touched on two issues that would be of major importance as the famine progressed. One was the rising price of food in Templecrone; the other was the major flaw in Prime Minister Peel's public works plan: namely, that it depended heavily on local landlords to guarantee that the money loaned by the government for public works would be repaid. Conyngham would not only refuse to guarantee repayment for public works, he absolutely refused to apply for them in the first place.

The rising price of food in Templecrone was an issue that created a great deal of bitterness in the parish during and after the famine. Rising food prices were viewed by the residents as profiteering by store owners who, they believed, were taking advantage of a beleaguered citizenry by charging exorbitant prices, knowing people had to buy food in order to survive, and therefore would pay any price, if they had the money.

And yet, the storekeepers had to raise prices for a number of reasons, none of them related to making a windfall profit on their merchandise.

First of all the scarcity of grain and potatoes created a very high demand for these foods, and this in turn led to suppliers of these commodities raising the prices they charged to stores because they knew that scarcity would give the stores no option but to pay the increased price. The store owners, in turn, passed these prices on to the consumer.

A second reason for the increased prices was that many of the stores sold these commodities on credit, and from experience the storekeepers knew that a considerable amount of the credit they extended would not be repaid, and so an increase in price was built in to compensate for this bad debt.

Finally, the storekeepers knew from experience that a famine destroyed their regular income, because they could not sell the volume of goods they sold in normal times, and therefore could not make their usual profits, and in order to compensate for a dramatic drop in the volume of business an additional sum was factored into the price so that the storekeeper himself could survive the crisis.

However, all these factored increases drove the price of potatoes and oats up by a 100% or even a 150%, and the customers who knew nothing about the dynamics of supply and demand, or even less about bad debts, suspected the storekeepers of racketeering, and very often the storekeepers were innocent of the charge.

Cornelius Ward was probably aware of much of this and hence his request to Captain Kennedy to bring shiploads of meal into the area was aimed at keeping prices down.

By the end of March of 1846, the situation throughout many parts of Ireland was getting desperate, and authorities believed that widespread violence would occur if people were not given work on Board of Works projects.

Delegations from around the country descended on Routh at Relief Commission headquarters demanding that employment be given immediately, but Routh told them that procedures had to be followed in order to get the projects under way.

The procedures laid out by Trevelyn were as follows: a Relief Commission of 5 had to be first formed in each area, comprised of two magistrates and three taxpayers. This Commission, in turn, could send a work and budget proposal to the Board of Works for repairing of roads, digging of drains, etc. The Board of Works then drew up its own work plans and estimates and sent them on to Trevelyn for review. The Central Relief Commission also reviewed proposals. Then the Board of Works sent out inspectors to inspect the project, who then wrote a report. If the project got an approval, a communication went to the Treasury, which in turn sent its comments to the Relief Commission, The Relief Commission then sent a final approval back to the Board of Works.[4]

The Board of Works had not nearly enough staff to cope with all these reports and the office was drowned in paperwork, as an avalanche of proposals came in from all over Ireland for review.

There were not enough inspectors to review projects in a timely manner, and there were not enough supervisors to go into the field and get the projects underway.

Then, of course, there were landlords like Conyngham who would have nothing to do with the Board of Works, and still other landlords, like Mrs. Gerrard of Ballinglass in Galway, who evicted 300 tenants on March 13, 1846, so she would not be responsible for them.

When there was widespread criticism in the newspaper over the evictions, Lord Broughman said in a speech in the House of Lords on March 23rd:[5]

"Undoubtedly it is the landlord's right to do as he pleased, and if he abstained he conferred a favor and was doing an act of kindness. If, on the other hand, he choose to stand on his right, the tenants must be taught by the strong arm of the law that they had no power to oppose or resist...property would be valueless and capital would no longer be invested in cultivation of the land if it were not acknowledged that it was the landlord's undoubted and most sacred right to deal with his property as he wished."

Riots erupted in Carrick-on-Suir and other major towns over the lack of food and lack of work, and the military and the police were sent in immediately to restore order.

The Lord Lieutenant threatened to hold up all aid if there were more public disturbances, and the British newspapers carried scare headlines about another Irish rebellion.

There was no violence in Templecrone in the spring of 1846, and no threat of it either, just a rising resentment at the inaction of the government and the total lack of government aid coming into the area.

This resentment simmered into anger as the people watched Russell empty the Conyngham grain warehouses, which had the last of the annual rents still stored there, and ship the grain and livestock taken in rent across to England.

Lord Brougham may have believed that men like Conyngham should be able to do as they pleased, but few in Templecrone would have agreed with him.

The major worry that Forster, Griffiths and other community leaders had at the beginning of April was that there would not be enough potato seed available for the 1846 crop.

Forster had expressed that fear back in December, when he urged tenants to save as much potatoes as possible for seed and to eat oats instead, but as relief was very slow in coming into the parish there were those who were driven by hunger to consume their seed, thus insuring they would have no food either for the following year. The situation was beginning to get desperate.

The Templecrone Relief Committee decided that getting seed to give the tenants was a priority and some of the funds that they acquired was diverted to this purpose.

The Mullaghderg Committee also sent out appeals for seed, and they too urged their friends and neighbors to save as much potato seed as possible for the spring planting.

Both groups had a short and a long-term problem that had to be solved.

The short-term problem was to get enough food to keep the people alive until the first new potatoes became available in June.

The long-term problem was to insure that enough seed potatoes went into the ground to insure that when the new crop became available it would be sufficient to carry the people through until the summer of 1847.

Neither committee ever considered the possibility of another failure in 1846, because such an occurrence would be unbelievable, and the consequences were too terrible even to think about.

The vast majority of the residents of the area believed that the crop failure of 1845 was like a lighting strike—it just struck once in a particular spot and never struck in that area again.

* * *

All through the first four months of the year Templecrone was battered with snow, hail and sleet mixed with torrential downpours. Thousands of hungry people huddled in waterlogged cabins, crowding around peat fires, praying for survival.

All of them thought relief would come with the early crop of potatoes in June. But salvation was much longer off than that, and for some there would be no salvation.

* * *

As spring stretched into summer, the resources of Relief Committees and the assistance given by friends were not enough to provide food for all of the families and the more desperate of these families began to sell anything that had a market value.

Beds, clothes and utensils were all offered up for sale by the destitute and any funds raised in this manner were immediately converted into food.

The families who were a level above the destitute began to eat their chickens, pigs, and cows, some of which were being saved for the rent, and those families who had already consumed their chickens and livestock, sold watches, rings and any other heirloom that could be turned into oats.[6]

In May and early June, those who had planted their potato seeds went off to Scotland, on borrowed money, to look for work. Some got work but many did not because Scotland was swamped with destitute Irish laborers looking for work, and there were ten men applying for every job that became available. These men were forced to apply for relief from the authorities in various towns in Scotland, and their presence was resented by the inhabitants of these towns who resented having to support these destitute Irish laborers.

Children as young as ten, both boys and girls, were herded off to Letterkenny and Ballybofey to the hiring fairs, where their parents would offer them to farmers from Derry or Tyrone as farm laborers and household help for the summer for a pittance wage.[7]

Many were hired, and were at least guaranteed food and shelter for the next six months, and their wages went for food for the rest of the family. However, many went home without a job, because the supply of labor far exceeded the demand, and the farmers recruited only the strongest. The weakest, who needed the work most, went home hungry.

Those that were not hired did something that would have been unthinkable the previous year: they begged for food from houses along the thirty mile stretch back to the Rosses. The pride and independence of these people was breaking down and it was a measure of their destitution that they were willing to beg in order to survive.

But most of the households along the way could offer little help, because they too were suffering from the same scarcity of food that was destroying the self-respect of the laboring families of the Rosses, and most of the Rosses laborers went back home without acquiring any food.[8]

Most of the early appeals for help issued by the Templecrone Relief Committee, or the reports written by the Quakers, emphasized the peaceful nature of the people, and time and time again Forster and Griffith stated that no matter what the hardship endured by the people they never even considered restoring to violence.

While this was true of the vast majority of the people, there were a few who did indeed resort to violence, if the provocation was great enough, and while this happened rarely, it did in fact happen. This violence, however, was not organized and was in response to a particular situation.

One of the occasions when local people reacted violently was on March 31, 1846, when a sloop named the Mariner came into Burtonport to buy a cargo of potatoes from Russell, Conyngham's agent. Russell had gathered up the potatoes in lieu of rent a few months earlier, and he intended to sell them to the skipper of the Mariner.[9]

Potatoes were as scarce as gold dust in the Rosses on March 31, 1846, and when word went around the parish that that potatoes were being shipped out of the area, some reacted with fury.

At 8:00 p.m., under cover of darkness, 20 men came on board the Mariner and beat up the captain and the crew, tore the rigging, and then tried to scuttle the ship in the harbor.

When this failed, they departed after telling the captain and the crew that they would lose their lives if they tried to leave Burtonport with a cargo of potatoes because they would be intercepted at sea and the ship would be sunk.

The raiders then took the ship's lifeboat, which they damaged and left it beached on the rocks at Inniscoo.

The attack provoked fear and rage among government officials who viewed it as a dangerous act of piracy and a threat to British control of the area. Reports, letters and other documents went back and forth from government headquarters about the incident. A reward was offered for the apprehension of the raiders, but they were never identified and the reward went uncollected.

The reaction of the British can only be understood when viewed in the context of Britain's methodology in maintaining law and order in Ireland. The British rulers of Ireland and their Anglo-Irish allies were never any more than a small minority of the population, and this small minority maintained its control by the instant use of force against any member of the majority who dared to oppose its rule.

The use of force or the threat of it was of special interest to the resident landlords or the agents of absentee landlords, who were very often surrounded by a Gaelic speaking Catholic population and the perception that all the might of the British government would come down on anyone who attacked a landlord was very often the only protection a landlord or an agent had.

In Templecrone, Forster was very vulnerable since he and his family lived among his tenants and could be attacked any time. Russell also lived among his tenants and was also very vulnerable, since he had no protection except for the police, many of whom were Catholic, and he believed he could not always rely on them.

Russell and Forster, therefore, relied on the fear local people had of massive retaliation, and this fear was great enough most of the time to keep the population docile. But Russell and Forster were students of Irish history and they knew that occasionally the pot boiled over, and if it did they could lose their lives.

So, the attack on the Mariner was a warning, and the warning made them nervous.

British officials had another reason for being upset about the attack, and this had to do with their laissez faire doctrine which the British had elevated to the level of a religion. The British believed that Conyngham had the absolute right—indeed a "sacred right" to do what he pleased with the potatoes in his possession: he could sell them, keep them or throw them away, and his tenants had no say in the matter, even if they were starving, and the idea that the people of Templecrone would dare to interfere with free trade was an attack on the British economic system, and was therefore a high crime, comparable to an insurrection.

The raiders, who probably came from the islands, Arranmore or Inishfree, were not out to attack the British Empire or torpedo the British economic system: they were just hungry, angry men who were furious that food was leaving the harbor while their wives and children starved.

* * *

In early April, Cornelius Ward and his Mullaghderg Committee sent a copy of the petition they had sent to the Lord Lieutenant to the *Londonderry Journal* and asked to have it published.[10]

The *Londonderry Journal* from time to time opened its pages to attacks on certain landlords who were mismanaging their estates, but these attacks were never engaged in because of any sympathy for the tenants who were the victims of this mismanagement, but rather because the mismanagement hurt the economy and also made other taxpayers, mainly the Anglo-Irish, responsible for feeding the destitute.

Conyngham had been a target of the *Londonderry Journal* since September of 1845, when the paper reprinted the Campbell Foster expose from the *Times*, so when Cornelius Ward sent along his petition, the paper printed the petition much to the annoyance of Conyngham and his agent Russell.

An unnamed correspondent to the *Londonderry Journal*, perhaps Russell, replied with a letter which stated that there was no destitution in Templecrone; that there was plenty of food in the parish; and that there were no men available to do work, implying that the men of Templecrone were too lazy to work[11].

A week later, another correspondent wrote a letter unsigned as was the custom of the time accusing the writer of the previous letter of being prejudiced, and suggested that the person was an individual who did not want any food sent to Templecrone. The writer stated that one third of the potato crop had been wiped out and Templecrone was staring famine in the face.[12]

As for the accusation that there were no men available for work, the writer stated that the vast majority of men were busy preparing the land for the spring crop of potatoes and therefore could not take on any other kind of labor.

Conyngham himself seems to have decided that it was time to do a little public relations on his own behalf and an item appeared in the *Londonderry Journal* on May 20th, which revealed that Conyngham had decided to build a Catholic church for the Reverend James Hargan, the priest newly assigned to Arranmore and also to give the priest a portion of land free. The item stated that Conyngham had directed Russell to provide these gifts for the Catholic Church. The item ended with the following:

"The noble Marquis has also instructed his worthy and kind hearted agent to provide food and employment for the poor on the estate, who are not to apply for relief if visited by distress, to any other fund."[13]

This particular communication had to have been sent in by Russell, since it is extremely doubtful that any resident of Templecrone would have described Russell as "worthy and kind hearted." And the idea that Conyngham was prepared to provide food and employment was an outright lie, since he had provided no such assistance up to this point and was giving every indication that in the months ahead that he was not going to give any assistance either.

However, Conyngham was feeling the unfavorable publicity, and this was his way of assuring the other Anglo-Irish landlords in Donegal that he was not such a bad person after all.

* * *

Meanwhile, Lord George Hill, who was a past master of public relations, was running ads in the *Londonderry Journal* inviting the gentlemen of the county to visit his newly refurbished hotel in Gweedore.[14]

Several years before Hill had written a self-serving book entitled *Facts from Gweedore* which described how he had bought a 20,000-acre rundown estate in 1838 and after rearranging all the holdings had created an estate that was a model for all Irish landlords.

All of Hill's claims had been accepted without question at the time and nobody raised the question of what happened to all the original tenants on the estate, who had been evicted.

An editorial in the May 20th edition of the *Londonderry Journal* lavished praise on Hill and his new hotel and described him as "The noble lord of the soil" who was "developing a wilderness" and improving the "social and moral condition of the people."

Hill had long been a pet of the editors of the *Londonderry Journal*, who contrasted his well-run estate with the dilapidated nightmare that was Conyngham's Templecrone.

Because of this, Conyngham was in the unhappy position that no matter what he did he could not get an ounce of credit out of this newspaper unless he had Russell put a letter in the letters section; Hill was in the happy position of being fireproof that he could do no wrong, because his book had made such an impact that it created a new reality for Hill's reputation that would last for decades.

The propaganda warfare that Conyngham and Hill were engaged in was fought against the backdrop of hunger and destitution that was increasing in both estates, and both were aware that their financial wellbeing was being threatened by the rising destitution.

Conyngham tried to protect his finances by spending nothing on relief and getting all the rents he could; Hill was shoring up his finances by promoting his hotel and also squeezing the last penny of rent out of his tenants.

Both landlords believed that conditions on their estates would improve with the early crop of potatoes arriving in June. Neither knew that the situation would get much worse before it got better.

* * *

As May of 1846 drew to a close the early crop of potatoes were blooming and it looked like there would be an abundant supply for the needs of the parish.

On the 28th of May, the constable in Dungloe, Henry Minchire filled out a questionnaire sent to him by the Relief Commission at Dublin Castle. The questionnaire was being used to gather information about the extent of the potato crop planted in Templecrone in 1846, and on the other crops if any, that had also been planted.[15]

The Inspector General, D. McGregor, who sent out the survey also wanted information on what percentage of the land was let in con-acre.

Con-acre was a system in which tenants with holdings of 5 to 10 acres let a portion of it, usually an acre, to a landless laborer who would set a potato crop on that acre. The tenant would also supply fertilizer to the laborer, and the laborer would pay the tenant with a portion of the potato crop.

The benefit for the tenant was that he could use his share of the con-acre crop to help feed his family and use other sections of his holding to grow barley or oats, which were given to the landlord for rent.

The benefit for the landless laborer was that it allowed him access to a plot of land, and this plot of land supplied him and his family with food, so that the con-acre practice in many cases was a matter of survival.

The survey that the Dungloe constable filled out contained three critical items of information. One was that a much bigger crop of potatoes had been set in 1846 than had been set in 1845; the second item was that no additional grain crops had been set in 1846; and the third item was that no land had been let in con-acre.

The huge crop of potatoes that had been set was an indication that the relief committees had somehow managed in early spring to get sufficient seeds into the hands of the people of Templecrone to insure that a bumper crop of potatoes would become available in the early summer.

However, the answers provided to questions 4 and 5 were such that they indicated that a radical change had taken place between 1845 and 1846, and these changes were a recipe for disaster.

Question 4 asked: "What proportion has been this year let in con-acre?" The answer was "none."

Question 5 asked: "What crops have been sown in the land which would, under ordinary circumstances, have been planted with potatoes?" The answer was "none but potatoes."

The absence of any land let in con-acre clearly indicated that the landless laborers who survived on the con-acre practice were not going to have crops in the bountiful harvest about to be yielded by the soil of Templecrone, and would, therefore, be worse off than the previous year.

But the fact that most of the land that could be cultivated was set with potatoes with apparently no additional barley, oats or wheat set at all, which was the landlord's crops, posed a potential disaster on two fronts: one, there would be no additional food at all if the potato failed; and two, there would be no way the rent could be paid if the potato failed and the people consumed the other crops for food.

The tenant farmers who set most of their land with potato seeds were planning to capitalize on the high price being paid for potatoes and the heavy demand that would be there once the potatoes began to be harvested in June.

No doubt they believed they would quickly make the landlord's rent by selling the potatoes, and have plenty of potatoes left to feed their pigs, chickens and children who thrived on this all-purpose food.

One can only wonder why these tenant farmers let none of their land in con-acre. Perhaps the reason for this was a wish to use all of the land to make windfall profits on the demand for potatoes, and the laborers may have been hired anyway to provide help on the farm, with the understanding that they would be paid in potatoes once the crops were harvested.

The Dungloe constable who signed his request gave no indication in his handwritten response that the answers to the survey foreshadowed the disaster that was to occur very shortly.

He was not the only one who could not foresee the future. All of Ireland, and all of Britain, had no inkling of what was about to happen either.

* * *

On June 3, 1846, the early potato crop suffered a total failure and this was followed by a total failure of the late crop, and the situation in Templecrone changed from being a time of extreme distress to a situation in which the entire community faced annihilation if a massive assistance program was not put into place with all possible speed.

Had the potato crop not failed in 1846, the hunger of the previous nine months would never have attracted any attention from historians, because such food shortages had been known in Ireland before.

But a total failure, all over Ireland, coming on the heels of the serious shortages of the previous season created a situation that posed the gravest threat to the survival of the Irish people since the Cromwellian wars two centuries before—wars which almost destroyed the Irish nation.

The acute shortage of food posed by the potato failure was made more life threatening by the poor physical condition of the people of Templecrone after a long, hungry winter.

Medical doctors who practiced in the area, Dr. Swan and Dr. Frazer Brady frequently described the ill health of many of the people, even when not threatened with famine. Malnutrition was widespread and the result was that most children were lucky to survive the first year of life, and those people who did manage to grow into adults had only an average life expectancy of 38.

Visitors to Templecrone before the famine, including O'Donovan and Mitchell, described hordes of beautiful children, as well as adults with weather-beaten and unhealthy faces, worn out from hard work and despair.

The food shortages of the winter of 1845 had no doubt a serious impact on the physical condition of the people, and more children than usual died that winter, and many tired adults gave up on living, years before their time.

Those who died in the winter of 1845 died from a variety of causes, but few deaths were from hunger and none were from the fever that was to devastate Ireland the following year. Stress caused these deaths: stress brought about by seeing fellow family members suffer; stress generated by the deaths of children; stress brought on by widespread despair.

While stress is rarely mentioned in connection with the famine, it may have carried off more people than hunger did, and it may even have been as deadly as the famine-related diseases which began in 1847.

The failure of the potato crop affected everybody in Templecrone, not just the destitute of the parish. Conyngham and Forster now faced the reality that their tenants were going to be poorer this year than they were the previous year and this could result in very real financial problems for these landlords.

The storekeepers who had advanced credit to many destitute tenants during the winter and spring would not get paid, indeed might never get paid, and not only that, they could be put out of business entirely since few in the parish would have money to buy anything in the stores.

As for the rest of the population, their only hope was to get help from charitable organizations or have the government begin public works projects immediately.

Conyngham's immediate reaction to this latest crisis was to put his estate up for sale. The following ad was placed in the *Londonderry Journal* and other publications on June 17th, just as the nature of the total potential crop failure became evident.[16]

ADVERTISEMENT
County of Donegal Ireland

To be sold, the Rosses Estate, consisting of nearly 40,000 acres, in one or three lots, to suit the convenience of the purchaser. It is situated in the Northwest coast of Donegal, in the Parish of Templecrone, and Barony of Boylagh, 24 miles each from the towns of Donegal and Letterkenny. The making of kelp, which has lately become so valuable for the making of iodine, gives profitable employment to thousands of both sexes and all ages during the summer months. There is an excellent house upon the estate, in which the agent to the property resides, and the tenants are mostly at will. An estate of such extent, and, in all respects so desirable has not, for many years, been offered for sale in the North of Ireland.

The ad then stated that agent Robert Russell would show prospective buyers the estate, and further particulars could be obtained from John Conwall, Esq., 36 Rutland Sq. Dublin or John Henry Benbow, Esq., No. 1 Stone Buildings, Lincoln Inn, London.

Conyngham, of course, hoped to make a fast exit from Templecrone, because it was evident to him that the estate could become a major liability in the coming year. And his fears were not without justification.

All over Ireland landlords who had forgiven rents and even borrowed money to help feed their starving tenants were now facing bankruptcy, and many of them did in fact go bankrupt during 1846.

Conyngham had no worry about going bankrupt because of borrowing money to help out his tenants; his main concern was that the British government would enact tough new legislation that would force Irish landlords to be completely responsible for their destitute tenants, and if such a law were passed and enforced he could indeed be faced with bankruptcy.

Conyngham had good reason to fear such a possibility. There was a rising clamor in the British Parliament against spendthrift Irish landlords and a willingness to make them pay the bill for Ireland's indigent.

Such laws had been threatened in the past, but Conyngham or his ancestors had not been afraid when George IV had been king, and a friendly government had been in power.

But this was a different age. The Catholics had the vote and were using it; Queen Victoria was not a close friend of the Conynghams'; there was a hostile Tory government in power; and not all the media had respect for "lords of the soil." Conyngham thought the time ripe to sell.

Forster took another approach but for different reasons. Forster had no power base except in Templecrone, and, unlike Conyngham, he did not have other estates and other revenues to fall back on, because his estate in Templecrone was all he had. He was a local entrepreneur without a title and without aristocratic ties and his fortune rose and fell with how well he managed his local estate.

So, in the absence of help from Conyngham or the government, Forster decided to go into the kelp business in a big way, investing money in harvesting the kelp, and hoping to save his estate by helping his tenants and other people in the area earn money.

One of the misrepresentations in the Conyngham ad for the sale of his estate was that there were "thousands" working in the kelp industry and implying that the Conyngham agent Russell was somehow involved in the employment of those thousands. The truth was that there had been hundreds involved in early 1846, not thousands, and Conyngham or his agent had nothing at all to do with this industry.

The way the kelp industry had been organized was that whole families were involved in harvesting the kelp all summer long, and local storekeepers had acted as wholesalers, assembling the kelp of scores of families into boatloads, which were then shipped to Britain. When the storekeepers got paid for the shipment, they then paid the families the payment often coming at the end of the summer.

Forster on the other hand, was willing to pay cash up front, and using superior business skills and better contacts was able to get a better price for the kelp, which benefited both him and the workers.

He was eventually able to get thousands involved in the industry, and while he saw that his own tenants got all the work they wanted, he put a great many of Conyngham's tenants to work as well. By doing this, Forster no doubt saved many lives, and prevented his own slide into destitution as well.

In spite of Conyngham's lofty promise in the *Londonderry Journal* on May 20th that he would give aid and employment to his tenants in time of need, Conyngham reneged right away as soon as disaster struck.

Conyngham stated that he was not able to help his tenants and was selling his estate because of personal financial difficulties.

Conyngham also moved to collect any rents he could, and Russell and his bailiffs were out on the bogs, islands and mountains, gathering up any livestock they could get in lieu of the six month rent which was then due, and putting a claim in on any field of oats, wheat or barley that had yet to ripen.

The tenants agreed to give all they had, because eviction was a death sentence, and the tenants would rather die within their own walls of hunger than die of exposure on the open roads.

So, Conyngham got everything that had not been eaten or pawned and his tenants were truly destitute except for the income from the kelp.

CHAPTER EIGHT

The Peel government fell on June 29, 1846, and was replaced by a Whig administration headed by Lord John Russell.

Russell was viewed as a liberal who was an advocate of civil and religious liberty, but he had little respect for Catholicism, and he was a solid champion of the absolute right of property owners to do what they pleased with their property.

Russell was the son of the Duke of Bedford and was arrogant about his aristocratic lineage. He was so small in stature, less than five feet, that he was ridiculed by his enemies as a midget, or as a girl, or as a mite. When he married the widow of Lord Ribbesdale, he was nicknamed "The Widow's Mite."

Russell had an Irish estate Ardsallagh Castle, County Meath, and his father had been the Lord Lieutenant of Ireland between 1806 and 1807. But he disliked the Irish, and considered the people a great burden on the British Empire.

However, while in Parliament he had initiated an investigation into the revenues of the Church of Ireland in 1834, much of which had come from a tithe of 10% that was imposed on all the Irish, including Catholics, and he initiated a debate in Parliament in 1844 on the mismanagement of Ireland, which drew attention to the plight of the Irish.

But those investigations were not initiated because of any wish of his to promote the interests of Irish Catholics, but were initiated because of his conviction that Ireland was owned by incompetent spendthrifts.

As soon as he assumed power, Russell made it clear that from that point onwards Irish property owners and taxpayers would foot the bill for all aid to the poor.

Russell gave Trevelyn dictatorial powers in Ireland, and Trevelyn in turn drew up a new plan to handle relief in Ireland.

Trevelyn's plan came in two segments: a Board of Works scheme, and a new relief scheme.[2]

The Board of Works plan was to be undertaken on a large scale, but unlike the plan initiated by the Peel regime, which provided some of the money as a grant, this plan called for the landlords and taxpayers to repay all the cost of Board of Works schemes in their area over a 10-year period at 3% interest. The Treasury, however, would advance the money for the schemes, but would only do so when the landlords asked for it and guaranteed repayment.

As for the relief scheme, Trevelyn said that the government would not interfere with private enterprise and would not buy any food for distribution. All food must be bought by local grain dealers, and the charitable organizations had to buy from the dealers in order to give to those who were destitute.

The only exception to this rule was certain remote and destitute areas on the west coast, like Erris and Templecrone, where government food depots would be stocked, but would not open until there was no food available from dealers. Even then, no matter how destitute the inhabitants of these areas, were even if they were dying of hunger, no food would be given away and must at all times be purchased.

Russell's new policies created an uproar among his political opponents and even among some of his supporters.

Irish landlords were furious that all the burden for coping with the catastrophe was being placed on them, and leaders of the Catholic community viewed the policies as an attempt at genocide.

The Marquis of Landsdowne said Ireland was the victim of "wicked laws" designed to make her poor, and then was blamed for her poverty. He said these laws were bringing her to the edge of a "vast monster grave" for the entire nation[3].

Lord Cloncurry said that Irish wealth was being taken out of Ireland by the English, and all Ireland was asking was to be allowed to keep some of this wealth during this terrible crisis[4].

Canon O'Rourke, author of *The Great Irish Famine*, a book published in 1874, took the British to task for being unwilling to spend money to buy food for the Irish, which would have cost relatively little and saved millions of lives.

"It was a question of money. The government would not advance enough money to buy the wheat, oats or barley grown in Ireland. England could find a hundred million [pounds] to spend in fighting the Grand Turk; she could find twenty million for the slave owners of her colonies; she could find twenty million more for the luxury of shooting King Theodore, but a sufficient sum could not be found to save the lives of five million of her own subjects."

O'Rourke had a point, if England had spent only 5 million pounds on the purchase of food in 1846 there would have been little hunger in Ireland.

* * *

Russell ignored all the critics, however, and gave Trevelyn the go ahead with his new scheme. Trevelyn ordered all relief committees to present schemes for Board of Works projects and told the landlords and taxpayers that they were responsible for repaying all the money for these schemes advanced by the Treasury.

Trevelyn, and his aide Routh, also informed the citizens of Templecrone that a food depot would be established at Burtonport but that they should look to local merchants for food supplies, since the depot would not be opened for the sale of food unless all local supplies were depleted.

* * *

Even though it was evident in both England and Ireland that the Irish were facing a major catastrophe, there was a great deal of resistance in leading English newspapers to give aid of any kind to Ireland.

An editorial in the *Times* stated that England was sick of the Irish begging for help "The false tears of a professional beggar. It is possible to have heard the tale of sorrow too often," observed the *Times* editorial, on August 3, 1846.

Punch, a prominent magazine, had cartoons running every week that portrayed the Irish as filthy, brutal assassins, begging for money which they then used to mount a rebellion.

"With the money they get from relief funds, they buy arms," one cartoon caption stated.

* * *

A general meeting of West Donegal landlords was convened in Donegal Town on the 7th of September in the courthouse, with representatives of the baronies of Tirhugh, Banagh and Boylagh present. Neither Conyngham nor his agent Russell were present, even though Conyngham was the largest landlord in the area. Francis Forster of Roshine Lodge was also absent.[5]

Colonel Conolly, who had a great deal of property in Lettermacaward and Inishkeel, the parishes south of Templecrone, played a leading role in the meeting, and he stated he would apply for Board of Works projects that the government said they might make available to destitute areas like West Donegal.

Conolly said he would not ask any small taxpayer on his property to share the burden, but he asked everyone who could afford it to donate money to the relief committees, so the poor of the area would not die of starvation.

Other landlords, like Alexander Hamilton of Coxtown, followed Conolly's lead, and the Protestant clergymen present promised to work to raise funds to buy food.

All present agreed that the destitute poor of West Donegal were not looking for free food, but only wanted to gain employment which would enable them to buy food for their families.

* * *

All during August and September of 1846 appeals for help continued to pour in to Routh in Dublin from Templecrone and the neighboring parishes of Lettermacaward and Gweedore.

On August 3rd, T.L. Molloy, a Church of Ireland clergyman who was head of the Lettermacaward Relief Committee informed Routh that the parish was without food and that the committee had only 30 pounds which was donated by Colonel Conolly. Molloy begged for assistance.[6]

John Rogers, secretary to the Lettermacaward Relief Committee wrote to the relief commissioners asking for a shipment of meal to be sent into Rutland since the people were without food, and the dealers had none either.

There was no reply from Routh.

On August 20th the Reverend Valentine Griffith, Chairman of the Templecrone Committee, wrote to William Stanley of the Central Relief Commission, Dublin Castle, asking that another shipment of Indian meal be sent to Burtonport because the previous shipment was all gone, and the price of oaten meal in the area had now doubled[7].

Griffith also demanded that public works projects commence immediately or that free food be given to the people of Templecrone, since many of them were starving and had no money to buy food at any price. If aid were not granted, he wrote, the destitute would either die or would all have to be sent to the poorhouse in Glenties, which could not accommodate them anyway.

So, help was needed immediately—as a delay could be fatal.

Routh wrote back that Griffith should apply for shipments of grain to regional headquarters in Sligo, and that he had passed the request for public works on to the appropriate authorities.

On August 24th a document was delivered to the Dungloe police barracks from Dublin Castle marked "strictly confidential." It was a request for information from D. McGregor, Inspector General, and was sent to John C. Rodden, sub inspector who was in charge of the Dungloe police barracks.[8]

McGregor had four questions.

1. Has the extent of the potatoes planted this year equaled that of ordinary years?
   The answer: more than equaled that of former years.

2. Has the crop been affected by the blight and in what proportions?
   The answer: All the potatoes are affected by the blight and rendered unsafe for food.

3. Has the early or late crop been chiefly injured and to what extent, in each of those crops?
   The answer: Ninety-nine parts out of one hundred of the early crop injured, and all the late crop rendered useless.

4. Has the crop, or any portion of it, as yet, become available for food?
   The answer: No part of this year's crop has become available for food.

One wonders what the point of this survey was since Griffith and Forster had already sent appeals to Dublin Castle about the total destruction of the Templecrone crop.

Perhaps the British authorities did not believe the reports coming out of Templecrone and others areas and were asking the police to double-check all reports.

In any case, it was very evident that Routh and the British government were made well aware of the extent of the destitution in August of 1846.

They might plead later that they were not aware of the extent of the catastrophe, but these police surveys, which were circulated all over the west, stated clearly the nature of the food shortages.

* * *

On Monday, August 31, 1846, a meeting attended by 2,000 people was held on the Fair Hill, Dungloe. The meeting was called by the Templecrone Relief Committee in order to let a desperate and restless people know what the committee was doing to get help for the area.[9]

Eyewitnesses at the meeting recalled how the majority of the people showed the effects of hunger and ill health, and despair was the most common expression on the faces of the people.

The Reverend Valentine Griffith chaired the meeting, and Francis Forster, Doctor Brady, R. K. Thompson, the Reverend McMenamin, the Reverend McDevitt, the Reverend Hargan, the Reverend Boyle, and Robert Russell was also on the platform.

Russell's presence on the platform was a surprise to some, but not a surprise to others.

Russell had been made very nervous by the attack on the Mariner on March 31st and he was probably afraid of being perceived as provocative if he stayed away from the meeting. And since Conyngham had failed to get a buyer for the estate, he was trapped in Templecrone and had to minimize the danger of living there.

Forster told the assembled masses he was doing everything possible to help the people, and most people believed him. He had 500 families working on processing kelp, which he was exporting to Scotland, and the money these families earned was enough to keep these families alive.

The Reverend Griffith spoke of his efforts to get donations to buy food, and he also spoke of his campaign to get Board of Works projects started in the area, which would give employment to the most needy.

Father McMenamin urged all present to have faith and to trust in God, and they would get through the crisis.

Then Russell got up and said that rents were being reduced 25%, and that Conyngham would do all he could, within his means, to help.

Russell's remarks were met with silence. Few had any means left to pay 10% of the rent, never mind 75%, and as far as Conyngham helping out, that would have to be seen to be believed.

Most people left the meeting confident that the parish would get assistance. Many were convinced that the British government would step in and give free food, and that it was only a matter of time before this happened.

But by August of 1847, a year later, dead bodies were piled outside a fever hospital in Dungloe that had been built on the site of the mass meeting the year before and the British had still not given away free food.

* * *

The Gaelic customs of reaching out to neighbors in trouble was adhered to during the winter of 1845/1846 and into the spring of 1846.

But with the total failure of the 1846 potato crop, this custom came under siege, because now nobody had potatoes and those who had other vegetables like turnips, cabbage or carrots had these vegetables as their only source of food[10].

The food left at the doors of needy families was not left there now and by the end of the summer only close relatives, aunts, uncles, and first cousins were sharing with one another.

The destitute were then forced to rely on the charity of the relief committees, which were not raising enough funds to feed all those who needed it, and they had to sell whatever assets they still had in order to get money for food.

Sheep, pigs, chickens and other animals still alive in the summer of 1846 were either sold and the proceeds used to buy oatmeal, or were actually slaughtered and eaten.

Family heirlooms, if they still existed, went next, and by September there were many in the parish who were totally destitute, without food or assets of any kind.

One option left was to walk sixteen miles to the poorhouse in Glenties, across the Gweebara River, but this was an option that was used only by the most desperate, since it was the ultimate shame for a Templecrone family to be reduced to this condition, and many even when faced with death by starvation would rather die in their own homes than face the humiliation of the poorhouse.

A primitive form of socialism also evolved in some areas as the distress deepened. My grandfather, Tim Gallagher, who was born in 1856 and died in 1956, said that his father, Bryan Gallagher of Ballintra, Arranmore, told him that he and several families who were relatives of his mother, Maura Green Gallagher, pooled all their resources and worked together for the common good.

Bryan Gallagher and the Greens—Daniel, Hugh, John and Michael—owned a total of 28 acres of good arable land in Ballintra, and when the potato crops failed in 1845 they had set some of the land in turnips, oats and carrots which turned out to be the only food they had in 1846.

Bryan Gallagher and the Greens also fished together in the small boats owned by the extended family. Each family had barrels of salted fish, which were used during the worst of the food shortages. Bryan Gallagher and the Greens provided neighbors with a great deal of help during the first crop failure, and help was also given during the second failure, but at a greatly reduced scale.

"My father always said that they gave what they could in 1846 but they had to make sure the family did not give it all way and then be as bad off as everyone else," my grandfather said.

"My mother was heartbroken at what happened during the famine, and she would eat very little because she couldn't stand the fact that there were people all around who had nothing while she had food.

"She never really got over what happened and it had an effect on her all her life, because she thought that some of the neighbors who lost relatives were angry at the Gallaghers and Greens because all of them survived."

* * *

Those who had a big crop of oats or turnips had to guard their crops as hunger became widespread in August and September of 1846.

Beggars from other areas, some as far away as Sligo and Mayo, found their way into Templecrone and began to take turnips out of fields that were not guarded.

Many farmers who had stores of food used dogs tied to a post in the fields to raise an alert if intruders were in among the oats or turnips. Other farmers had members of their families on guard duty all night. ·

Some of those caught were brutally beaten; others were let off with threats of punishment[11].

Stealing by one neighbor from another was very rare, but it was not unknown. One man in Aranmore caught a neighboring woman stealing his grain and attacked her with a scythe, cutting off her ear.

* * *

The poaching of fish and wild fowl became widespread as the food shortage became more acute.

Conyngham had bailiffs whose job was to make sure his tenants did not take trout from his streams and lakes, which he considered to be as much his property as the fields and bogs.

Condy Boyle, an officious bailiff who lived in Dungloe, was very energetic at enforcing the no fishing or hunting laws but when he tried to enforce them in 1846, he was met with furious opposition and he backed off.

Boyle was detested and feared, but he appeared to have no fear of the tenants, and this lack of fear was based, no doubt, on the fact that up until this point no landlord, agent, or bailiff had been attacked on Conyngham's estate.

Some of the local merchants ran into deep financial difficulties because of the potato failure in 1846 and a few of them went out of business entirely.

Johndy Sweeney, my great, great grand uncle, had been a fur trapper on the Missouri River for many years and had become wealthy in the process.

In 1842, while in his forties, he had returned home and a marriage was arranged between him and the teenage daughter of John Sweeney, a cousin, who owned Sweeney's Hotel, Dungloe.

Sweeney's Hotel was in decline at the time and its owner offered the hotel to Johndy Sweeney if he married John Sweeney's youngest daughter and spent some of his fortune fixing it up. Johndy agreed.[12]

Several months after the wedding, and with his young wife pregnant with the first of their twelve children, Johndy took off again for Missouri, but returned in 1844 with additional money to renovate the hotel.

In the year that followed he opened up a grocery store, began to buy knitted goods from local women, bought and sold kelp, eggs, and livestock and was renovating the hotel.

In 1845, with the partial failure of the crop, Johndy gave easy credit to a great many people, giving them potatoes, oats, and even dried fish on the understanding that they would repay him in the summer of 1846 when the new crop arrived.[13]

But when the potato failed in 1846 and the local economy collapsed, Johndy was left with a hotel that few visited and a mountain of credit slips that could not be collected, and his entire business came to a standstill.

Sweeney did not go out of business, however, because he had enough assets to keep him afloat, but the fur trapper who had arrived home from Missouri with high hopes of building a great hotel in the wilderness went very close to losing it all because of the failure of the potato crop in 1846.

As the winter of 1846/47 approached, the vast majority of people in Templecrone had exhausted all of their resources and were surviving on the food provided by the relief committees or on the handouts of other charitable organizations.

Those who could find work used the extra money to buy additional food; those who could harvest seaweed also used these earnings to buy food for their families. Those who were totally dependent on the food handed out at the relief centers supplemented their food allowance in any way they could, and this very often involved eating animals, birds and plants that would never have been eaten otherwise.

The need to supplement food given in charitable handouts was a vital one, because this food, such as soup, did not prevent starvation, it merely prolonged it, and the walking skeletons who shuffled around the roads of Templecrone in December of 1846 were a graphic illustration of this.

The supplemental food consumed by the people included edibles that would never be consumed in normal times but were consumed as hunger increased and the specter of death approached for those who had no other source of food.

When the potato stocks ran out on those who lived along the Templecrone coastline, those who never normally caught fish in order to eat them scrambled to acquire hooks and twine and the type of bait that would attract fish.

As the great hunger progressed, the rugged shores were crowded with people casting lines into the choppy sea in an attempt to catch a fish, any fish. Those who already had boats were farther out, and the amount caught in this way, while relatively small, was enough to fend off death from day to day.

People who lived miles inland, in the hills beyond Dungloe, in Meen Na Mara, Crovehy, and Thor, who had never fished in the sea in their lives, also trudged down from the mountains and cast their lines and were grateful for anything they caught. It was a proud man indeed who would arrive home with a 10-pound fish to a family who had eaten nothing for days, and the fish was boiled or roasted over the open fire and all of it was consumed: head, tail, fins, and guts. Nothing was wasted.

The seashore itself provided a harvest for those who knew what to look for. But among the edible shellfish and edible seaweed were shellfish and seaweed that could make those who ate it at the wrong time of the year, or without the necessary preparation, very sick, and given the weakened state of the people, ptomaine poisoning could be a death sentence.

During low tide the sea retreated out of Dungloe Bay all the way to Innishean Island, enabling the hungry families of the area to forage all over the sands, picking up all kinds of shellfish scattered around, deserted by the waters. Small crabs marooned in pools were snatched up and later turned into soup, and fluke, trapped in bigger pools, were hunted down and beaten or stabbed to death.

Cockles, mussels, and winkles were a major target and were taken from the places they were anchored to and thrust into bags. Edible seaweed was also grabbed up and bundled, and one member of the family always guarded the treasure trove of seaweed, in case some desperate person made off with it.

However, in early 1847, as the numbers foraging for shellfish and seaweed along the coastline increased, the amount of shellfish uncovered by each ebbing tide decreased, and by the spring of 1847, the beaches of Templecrone yielded very little food and the hungry inhabitants were forced to find other less appetizing diets to appease their hunger.

Desperate people will do desperate things, and the victims of hunger now turned their attention to all living things that could be turned into a meal of sorts, no matter how unappetizing.

The carcasses of sheep and cattle that had died of disease were eaten by people desperate for food. Normally the carcasses of such animals would have been buried promptly, but now great chunks of them were hacked off and hauled away to be turned into stews or soup. It is not known how many died from eating tainted meat, but there must have been some, although the relatives of such casualties would never have admitted that these deaths were the result of such an activity, and would have attributed the deaths to some other cause.

Although rabbits were not a favorite food of any local people except the desperately poor, they were stalked, cornered, and consumed. At first, the people along the sandy banks of Keadue, Maghery, and Carrickfin would set snares for the rabbits and trap them one by one. But, as time went by, hundreds of hungry people would come with picks and shovels to the areas where the rabbits had their warrens and they would dig down into the soft earth and corner the rabbits in their hiding places, taking scores at one time. Over a period of time they made the rabbits as scarce as cockles and mussels on the seashore.

The birds of the area were also hunted and attacked with stones or sticks, or were trapped on the ground by scores of ingenious booby traps. The eggs the birds laid in their nests were also taken whenever they were found, and chicks were not spared either. However, killing birds took a great deal of skill, and since there were so many of them around, they were never really in danger of being exterminated.

Foxes, which were never that plentiful in Templecrone, practically vanished as they were hunted down and killed, and other small animals, like hares, frogs, and eels met a similar fate.

As the shellfish and wildlife vanished from the area, the hungry people turned to plants and weeds not usually eaten and these then became the food needed to sustain life.

The poorer people of Templecrone in hungry times in the past had known which of the abundance of weeds growing all over the landscape were edible and which were not, and this knowledge was handed down from generation to generation.

Thus, it was known that the dandelion was edible and so were the roots of fern, and these could be boiled and turned into a nourishing, if somewhat bad tasting, broth.

Cress from the waterlogged bogs also made a nourishing dish, and so did the leaves of dock. Best of all were the despised nettles, which were sought out by everybody because they made a tasty soup. Legend has it that the nettles gathered in graveyards grew taller and stronger than anywhere else, and the graveyards of the area were picked clean of them.

Nuts and berries of all types were searched for and were picked and eaten on the spot.

Turnips and cabbage, which were fed to animals when there were potatoes in abundance were now consumed with relish and were cooked with other foods, like nettles or cress, in a vegetable stew.

All of these weeds and berries and wildlife consumed during the height of the famine saved many lives, because in areas where people did not know how to forage for them, or where these plants were not available, the death toll was much higher.

Indeed, the very poverty that plagued Templecrone for a long time had taught residents of the area how to survive in times of hunger, so that when the great hunger engulfed the parish they were able to use the survival skills handed down for generations. While this did not save the very old and the very young from death, it saved a great many other younger people and kept the death count at a relatively low level throughout 1846 and into early 1847.

CHAPTER NINE

In early October of 1846, the Templecrone Relief Committee, decided to print a circular, which was designed as a dramatic plea for help. The circular was also designed to put pressure on the government to honor the promises made by the Russell government when it took power in July. The Russell government had promised that food depots would be opened in areas like Templecrone, but so far no depots had been opened.[1]

The circular was distributed all over Britain and Ireland and was signed by Alexander Montgomery, Rector; Valentine P. Griffith, Officiating Minister; James McDevitt, P.P.; Francis Forster, Justice of the Peace; R. K. Thompson, Inspecting Officer of the Coast Guard; and G. F. Brady, Medical Superintendent.

The first paragraph of the document accuses the government of breaking its promises to Templecrone.

"It has been shown by the government valuation that the parish of Templecrone, generally called 'the Rosses,' situated on the Northwestern shores of Donegal, is the very poorest in this extensive county. Such a sad distinction had for a while one advantage: that the place would necessarily have attached there to precedence, when relief was dispersed; and the assurance which has been propagated, that the government had arranged and guaranteed to supply directly the poorest districts with food, helped us to hope, that we would be compensated for our melancholy notoriety, by falling into the hands of a considerate and merciful government. But these pledges and prospects seem not to be in the way of being realized."

The document goes on to describe the remoteness of the area, the total dependence on the potato, and the lack of any financial support from either the landlord or merchants.

"In such a frightful emergency this appeal is made; and it is sent forth in the lively hope that the case of the poor sufferers of Templecrone will command itself to, and engage the sympathy of benevolent Christian hearts. No other source or refuge can be thought of, for the place is far too unpromising, insignificant and miserable for merchants or capitalists to mind it; but the people are worthy for whom it should be done, having ever been peaceable, orderly and patient."

The document then stated that the poor people of the area shared with each other all they had and now they had nothing.

"Our case is urgent—a crisis is approaching, very many are passing tedious days, wandering about for relief destitute, afflicted, and tormented."

The Dungloe appeal generated a great deal of attention and there was a fresh surge of donations, but it made enemies of Trevelyn and Routh who did not take too kindly to having their integrity questioned in this manner.

* * *

Conyngham also disliked this new publicity on the destitution of his tenants and he had Benbow write a letter to the *Times*, which was published on October 4th. Benbow stated that Conyngham had put his estate up for sale earlier in the year in the hope that some rich investor would buy it and that the investor would be able to help the tenants more than Conyngham could. Benbow claimed Conyngham had no money; would get no rents from the estate that year; and had already reduced his rents by 38%.
Eight days later, on October 12th, Conyngham also wrote a letter to the *Times* in which he stated that he had borrowed heavily against the Templecrone estate and had a huge mortgage, which he could not pay now because he was not getting rents and he repeated what Benbow had stated he had no money.
Conyngham's position did not go down too well m Donegal, even among the Anglo-Irish gentry.
The *Ballyshannon Herald*, a weekly newspaper circulated among the Anglo-Irish, called Conyngham's claims "shameful" that he had plenty of money and just did not want to spend any on his tenants. The paper demanded that Conyngham do his duty, like Colonel Conolly and other landlords in the area, and stop crying poverty.
In 1846, Conyngham had over 170,000 acres of land in estates in Kent, England, in Donegal, County Clare, and Meath and an income of over 50,000 pounds—about $10 million in today's currency. He also had one of the most luxurious castles in Ireland at Slane, County Meath, as well as another country mansion in Kent, and a townhouse in London.
Conyngham mixed in the highest social circles and threw banquets regularly at his various abodes, and while it may have been true that his affluent lifestyle cost him more than his income, he had the ability to cut

costs, sell some of his property and pay off his debts. He certainly wasn't poor, and because he had a great deal of assets, he was legally bound by the Labour Rate Act to provide public works projects for his tenants.

But Conyngham was unmoved by those arguments and continued to resist all attempts to get him involved in famine relief.

* * *

In October, on the Hill estate, Hill presented awards to the most productive tenants on his estate. The cash awards had been donated by an English bible society, and they were given out in spite of the widespread destitution in Gweedore.[2]

Hill said he was well aware of the mood of the people and had only to look at them to see the effects of the destitution, but the money had already been provided for this purpose and the people might as well accept it.

The awards were given out in silence, and the crowd quietly dispersed when the ceremony was over.

Those who received cash awards immediately went to the grain store in Bunbeg and bought oats with their prizes.

* * *

On October 21st, the Reverend Valentine Griffith wrote again to Randolph Routh asking when he could expect relief to arrive in Templecrone to the food depot[3].

He stated that he did not know whether the government was deliberately withholding food, but that he was heartsick at the way people were being treated. Promises had been made, but promises were not being kept, and a great tragedy was unfolding.

There is no record that Routh responded to that letter.

Griffith wrote again on October 28th, asking Routh for seed for next year's crop. He informed Routh that getting seed was imperative if any food was to be grown in the parish in 1847.[4]

Routh took a month to reply and then he wrote that he would have more information about the seed at a later date and would write to Griffith then.

During October, a series of pleas came from Gweedore from Reverend Hugh McFadden, the parish priest.[5]

He claimed that Hill and other Gweedore landlords had not put in for public works and without public works thousands would die of hunger. He asked for food to be sent to Gweedore right away.

Routh replied that there was plenty of food in Letterkenny, 30 miles away and that McFadden should try to buy food there.

McFadden wrote back—furious—stating that Letterkenny was separated from Gweedore by a range of mountains, and anyway the people had no money to buy food there. They needed work.

Routh wrote back statin he was not in charge of the Board of Works, that McFadden should address his complaints to that department, and that it was pointless to keep asking for free food. It was against government policy. In October Routh also ignored appeals from Hill and other Gweedore residents.[6]

In early November Francis Forster sent a personal appeal to Dublin Castle asking for help in opening two soup kitchens in Arranmore Island and four on the mainland.[7]

He stated that the strength of the people was ebbing away and the only way to save their lives was to provide them with food.

He pointed out that Conyngham had stated in the *Times* that he was not in a position to help his tenants, so unless the government helped all was lost.

There was no reply on record from Routh to this plea.

On December 9th, Conyngham wrote to the *Times* informing the British public that he was reducing his rents once more. Since few rents were being collected, this was another public relations ploy by Conyngham.

* * *

In late November and early December wave after wave of snow swept across Northwest Donegal, the worst in living memory. It was accompanied by high winds and the whole area was buried beneath a deep white blanket.

All the stricken tenants in the mountain cabins were trapped and buried in the blizzard of snow, and during this period the death toll in these hovels began to mount, as the old and the very young succumbed to exposure and malnutrition.

During this time, typhus made its appearance also, and this disease and other diseases that accompanied the famine began to wreak havoc on the inhabitants of Templecrone, who, up until this point, had been warding off death by starvation.

It was into this deadly snow-covered environment that Quaker investigator James H. Tuke arrived on the 13th of December, 1846, to witness firsthand the destitution of Templecrone and report back on it to the Society of Friends headquarters in Dublin.

Tuke was an angel of mercy, because it was his reports, and the reports of other Quakers, which eventually started a flow of food into the parish, and put the spotlight on the horrible tragedy that was taking place in Templecrone and other areas of the west.

Tuke's credibility enabled fund raising efforts to get going in the United States on a large scale and headed off a disaster that could very well have annihilated the Irish people.

But neither Tuke nor anyone else could stop the wildfire spread of disease that was to claim 10 times as many lives as hunger, and in some areas of Mayo destroyed whole villages.

Tuke visited Dungloe on December 14, 1846, and stated that it was the most miserable village he had ever seen. He said there was not a pound of meal in the village and yet the street was full of people from the countryside crying with hunger and cold.[8]

The scenes Tuke was describing took place outside of Sweeney's hotel and outside Hanlon's hotel, the hotel I was born in a century later.

Tuke talked to Griffith and Forster and they told him that even worse conditions existed up in the hills and on the islands. They said only an immediate supply of food on a massive scale would head off a catastrophe.

Tuke then went to the poorhouse in Glenties, where he saw naked people, the sick and the dead all lying together in filth on straw in unheated buildings. He stated that the filth was unbelievable and the death toll among those who had sought refuge in this place was extremely high.

Tuke left Templecrone and Glenties, determined to get assistance there as soon as possible.

Before help arrived, at the beginning of January, 1847, blizzards dumped new mountains of snow on Northwest Donegal, and the dying continued in the isolated sod huts of Templecrone.

* * *

The visit to Northwest Donegal made by Tuke in December of 1846 began to bring results in January of 1847.

The report he had written on his travels in Templecrone and other areas of West Donegal was widely circulated among newspapers and among members of the Society of Friends in both Britain and Ireland and fund raising began immediately and food was purchased in Britain and sent in to the afflicted areas.

In London, affluent Quakers donated more than 4,000 pounds in late December, and Friends in Liverpool donated 2,000 pounds in the same week. Irish Quakers in America began a vigorous fund raising campaign for food, clothing and cash, and the donations flooded in.[9]

Provisions and boilers for soup kitchens were shipped out of Liverpool for the West of Ireland on board the Waterwitch, the Albert and the Scourge in January, and 30 barrels of Indian meal, 42 bags of rice, 69 sacks of biscuits, 40 sacks of peas, 4 sacks of Scotch barley, 10 casks of American beef, and six boilers to make soup were dropped off at Burtonport. Two of the boilers were sent into Arranmore and four were set up in other parts of Templecrone, including one in Burtonport, one in Annagry, one in Keadue, and one in Dungloe.[10]

This was an initial supply that did not even begin to meet local needs but it was welcomed by the starving people, who waited patiently in long lines to get a bowl of the soup made from the variety of provisions which had been dropped off. The initial supply was gone within a week and the pangs of hunger returned as the destitute waited for the next shipment.

In January, Forster and Griffith applied for a public works scheme to fix the roads in Templecrone and asked Conyngham to sign the application. He refused, saying he had no money.

Forster and Griffith said they had no money either, but signed for a loan of 3,000 pounds, which would be used to fix roads on the mainland and on Arranmore. Thousands applied for work on these roads, but only the neediest were given jobs.

The pay was eight pence per day, and the jobs were given mostly to men with families, or to widows with families, or to children who had lost their parents to hunger or disease. There were 240 pence per pound thus one pound guaranteed 30 days labor for one man, and 3,000 pounds could support 3,000 laborers for 30 days. The work was done periodically, so that the 30 days per person was stretched out over 4 months.

In spite of the aid coming into Templecrone the amount of food entering served only to slow down the progress of starvation, not eliminate it, and there were those desperate enough to steal the grain in the government store in Burtonport, in spite of the severe penalties imposed if they were caught.

On January 1, 1847, Thomas Gem, who was in charge of the government store reported to sub inspector Rodden, of Dungloe, that the store had been broken into during the night and three bags of Indian meal stolen. Gem believed that the bags had been loaded in a boat on the pier, several yards away, and the culprits escaped by sea.[2]

This was viewed as an "outrage" by the authorities, and a major investigation was launched, but nothing came of it.

Forster wrote two letters to the Lord Lieutenant in January, one containing a list of donations to the relief committee to provide aid for Arranmore; the other a list of donations for aid to the mainland[12].

Forster was getting increasingly bitter with the Lord Lieutenant, claiming that many were dying and nobody of influence seemed to care. He said he and his family had extended themselves beyond reason to collect all they could, but people were still dying of starvation.

Forster had a legitimate complaint: if the Quakers had not supplied food would the government have allowed the people of the area to die of hunger? It seemed clear that the government would still not have acted.

The Templecrone list of subscriptions was 60 pounds: 25 pounds from the British Relief Association; 15 pounds from Quakers in Britain; and 20 pounds from the Belfast Ladies Association.

The Arranmore list of subscribers donated 65 pounds: 4 pounds from Forster himself; 10 pounds from Reverend Alex Montgomery, the Church of Ireland Rector; 5 pounds from Father McMenamin and 5 pounds from Father McDevitt; one pound from Thomas Gem of Burtonport; 15 pounds from the Belfast Ladies Association; and from the Marquis of Conyngham—25 pounds—his first and only donation to his starving tenants.

The installation of soup kitchens in central areas drew people from the surrounding areas to get their share of the soup.

My father told me that his grandmother, Mary Campbell, of Cnocnagerrah, outside Dungloe, used to see a steady stream of people marching past her door every morning on the way into Dungloe to line up for the soup.

The Campbells, like the Gallaghers and Greens in Arranmore, came from an extended family who worked together, and they had some food all through the famine and even had sheep on the hillside behind their home.

The Campbells did not join the lineup for food every morning, but some of the people who passed their door, either going to the soup kitchen or coming from it, would knock and ask for alms. These people knew the Campbells were not destitute because they could see the sheep on the hillside.

Before the famine, and even during it, it was very rare that people would beg in their own parish. If they were reduced to begging they would go to a place far away, like Tyrone. But some were desperate, and when they knocked on the door, they were given a turnip, or a carrot, or a small amount of oatmeal, and then they went away. Rarely was a request for food made at my great-grandmother's door—the beggar just knocked and stood there, and my great-grandmother handed over the food without a word.

The Campbells were not unscathed by the famine years, however. Mary Campbell's parents, Mary and Patrick Ward, who lived above them on the hillside, caught the fever and died. Today, there is a ruin of an old house in the general location where the Ward homestead was, and beside it, according to local legend, is the unmarked grave of a man and woman who died of the fever.

Those who live near the ruins do not know the surname of the couple in the grave, and when I visited it I wondered if it was the grave of my great-great-grandparents. But I have no way of knowing for sure.

* * *

The fever which killed my great-great-grandparents was typhus, the most deadly of the many diseases that are generally called "famine fever."

Typhus had been common in Ireland for centuries, but it was only when there was destitution that the disease took on epidemic proportions.

The Irish and British knew there was a link between the fever and famine conditions, but the medical profession at the time did not know what the link was—all they knew was that when famine came, fever followed on its heels.

The carrier which was responsible for the wildfire spread of typhus was the common louse. Lice had always been present in Ireland, but they did not breed rapidly if people kept themselves and their homes clean. However, during the famine, people neglected personal cleanliness, and also crowded together in poorhouses and soup kitchens, and lice grew explosively on unclean bodies and then jumped from one body to another as people huddled together.[13]

When a louse bit a human with typhus, the louse got typhus too, and when it jumped onto another human and bit that human, the typhus was transferred to the other human. At the height of the epidemic, police, doctors and clergymen, who were neither unclean nor destitute, became infected by getting too close to people who had infected lice on their bodies close enough for a louse to get on their clothing.

It is possible the Wards became infected by one of the fever victims who came to Mary Campbell's door looking for alms while they were present. Thus an act of kindness by their daughter resulted in death for the parents.

* * *

Typhus attacks the small blood cells of the body, especially in the skin and brain, and poor blood circulation is a result. The face swells up, the complexion becomes dark, and the temperature rises. When the temperature gets very high, the patient begins to rave, twitch and throw himself about, and when delirious will throw himself into a lake or into the sea to cool down. This very often led to a drowning. Rashes, sores and gangrene follow, with the loss of fingers and toes, and a horrible odor emanates from the entire body, as if the body were already decaying, even before death.

Most of the people of Templecrone who caught the fever refused to go to the fever hospital in Glenties because they believed that anyone who went there never returned alive. There was much truth to this because conditions in Glenties were guaranteed to bring on death—no food, medicine, and the dead and dying huddled together.

It was widely known that typhus was contagious, and once people got it they became isolated, even from their own families. Some families in Templecrone built a fever shed beside their shack, and the patient was put in there to live, or die, alone.

Because of the fear of infection, people were reluctant to handle dead bodies, and corpses were buried beside the house, in the back garden in order to avoid carrying them miles to a graveyard.

* * *

Another fever designated as "famine fever" was known as relapsing fever, also transmitted by the louse. This fever was characterized by high temperature, vomiting, sweating and jaundice. Sometimes called yellow fever, the disease was not as deadly as typhus, but it could return several times hence it was named relapsing fever.

Other diseases like dysentery, bacillary dysentery, were brought on by eating old cabbage leaves, raw turnips or half- cooked seafood, and they, too, attacked much of the population.

Famine dropsy hunger oedema was evident in 75% of those who were starving, with children blown up like balloons, and limbs swelling and bursting.

The people of Templecrone who were under siege from hunger and disease, turned into walking skeletons, with skin falling in folds, and every bone in their bodies showing. The eyes of the victims sunk into their head, and heads appeared to be skulls covered in parchment. Teeth fell out, and the jaws of children protruded. The very young lost their voices and they neither laughed nor cried, but appeared to be in a stupor. As the condition of the children worsened, they began to look like little old men and women of 80, who belonged to a species of ancient midgets. At this stage death was often inevitable, because they would no longer respond to food or medicine.

* * *

Two new charitable organizations came on the scene in early 1847, each of which had a major impact on famine relief in Templecrone. One was the British Relief Association; the other was the Belfast Ladies Association.

The British Relief Association was founded in London in December of 1846 and had its first meeting on January 1, 1847.

The organization was described at the time as comprising a dozen merchant princes who met every day to raise funds for food, clothing and fuel for those who were not being assisted by the government.

Among the merchant princes were Baron Lionel de Rothschild, Abel Smith, Thomas Baring, J. Pim, of Pim's of Dublin, and Stephen Spring Rice.[14]

When Trevelyn was informed about the formation of the organization, he said the group was wasting its time because there was so much anti-Irish animosity in Britain that it would be difficult or impossible to raise funds for the relief of Ireland.

But the group paid no attention to Trevelyn and went ahead with its effort anyway, and over the next two years more than 470,000 pounds was raised, 40,000 pounds of which went for the relief of destitution in Scotland.

Most of the assistance given in Ireland by this organization was directed at the west of Ireland, and Templecrone was a particular beneficiary, because at one period in late 1847 and early 1848 almost 4,000 children were receiving one meal a day from the association. Without that help hundreds of children would have died.

* * *

The Belfast Ladies Association also had its first meeting on January 1, 1847, and the circular issued by the organization focused mainly on conditions in Donegal, especially in Templecrone.[15]

Extracts of letters written by James Tuke and William Forster who had surveyed Templecrone were included in the circular, as well as appeals from Francis Forster and Dr. George Frazer Brady.

"Starvation appears inevitable," wrote Tuke and William Forster. "The patience and goodness of these Donegal peasantry is unequaled. They never beg and never complain, but silently bear their sorrows in calm resignation."

Francis Forster also wrote a moving appeal on behalf of the suffering people of the parish.

"I hope through the exertions of my friends, to be able to save the lives of some; but many, many must die as English cholera has now commenced in every direction. Those who lived in the mountains, having consumed all their little oat crop have come down to the shores, in hope of keeping themselves alive by what they can get off the rocks. I have seen endless wretchedness: persons reduced to such a state of weakness by disease and insufficient food, as to be unable to leave their cabins; young mothers, with infants in their arms, dying from want of proper nourishment.

"Death is at all times awful, but death by starvation is doubly awful so slow, yet so certain old and young, all likely to meet the same fate."

Doctor Brady had sent a letter apologizing for being unable to attend the meeting because of the medical catastrophe already widespread in Templecrone. He gives a written description of the scene in one home he had visited:

"The aged parents had just fallen victims to the foul disease, and being carried to their final rest; their son, a husband and father, too, prostrated by the hand of pestilence, as well as famine, calls for food or something to cool his parched lips but asks in vain from the living and loved partner of his bosom; she has naught to give; she strains her infant to her breast, who seeks for nourishment from a polluted fountain, and, in the vain hope of stilling the cry of another and an older child, she bares the same bosom to it."

The pleas for help from Brady, Francis Forster, Tuke and William Forster did not fall on deaf ears: the Belfast Ladies' Association, which was composed mainly of Protestants, donated generously to the destitute of Templecrone, and in the following two years continued to send food and clothing into the area[15].

* * *

Meanwhile, on January 11th, Lord George Hill, of Gweedore, sent out a desperate plea for help for his tenants. Hill's Gweedore tenants were in the same condition as Conyngham's tenants and Hill was now desperate.[16]

"They are all of them in a starving condition, few having more than one scanty meal in the twenty-four hours. On this account, together with the very unwholesome nature of the food, severe dysentery has broken out, and is daily hurrying numbers into eternity.
"There are, as yet, no public works going on, and when they are proceeded with, only a limited number of hands will be employed.
"This appeal, then, is made to the sympathies of a kind and benevolent public, to enable the people to purchase Indian meal at the government stores, at a reduced price."

* * *

On January 12th, Reverend Valentine Griffith wrote to Dublin Castle pleading for help.

"I beg most urgently to request that you will forward with the least possible delay fifty tons of rye and fifty tons of oats. If these supplies are not sent here at once I am apprehensive what will happen."[17]

Routh wrote back to say that he did not have this amount of supplies and even if he had, there would have been no way to send them on expeditiously. The Templecrone Committee might try Longford (150 miles away) as supposedly there was grain there.

Dublin Castle, of course, was receiving a blizzard of letters from every parish in Ireland looking for help, all claiming to be as destitute as Templecrone, and the Central Relief Committee had never made any attempt to get organized in a way where meaningful help could be given because Trevelyn just did not want the British government to get into the business of feeding Ireland's poor regardless of the consequences.

So the desperate pleas from Templecrone, like the desperate pleas from other areas, were destined to go unanswered, and the only people who stood between the destitute of Templecrone and death were the Templecrone Relief Committee, the Quakers, the British Association, and the Belfast Ladies Association.

CHAPTER TEN

British government relief administrator Charles Trevelyn finally admitted publicly in January of 1847, that Ireland was in the middle of a very serious famine, but he refused to concede that the primary responsibility for dealing with the famine was with the British government. As far as he was concerned, this was a problem for the private sector.

In a conversation with Henry Kingscote, a member of the British Association, he said: "This is a real famine, in which thousands and thousands of people are likely to die." However, Trevelyn was not about to rush in and help. "If the Irish once find out there are any circumstances in which they can get free government grants," he said, "we shall have a system of mendacity that the world never saw."

Trevelyn had another reason for wanting to let the famine run its course without interference: he said he believed that God was punishing the Catholic Irish and he should not interfere with God's will.[1]

On February 1st, in a reply to a begging letter from a Colonel Douglas, a relief inspector, he wrote:

"We deeply sympathize with you and other officers who daily have to witness scenes of heart-rending misery without being able to give effective relief, but we must do all we can and leave the rest up to God."[2]

In another letter, Trevelyn said the knowledge that the famine was the will of God provided him with a consolation and he hoped that the Catholic priests were letting the people know that what was happening to them was an edict from above. The people should know this and should be told that they "are suffering from an affliction of God's providence."[3]

There were a number of Christian fundamentalists who shared Trevelyn's views and wanted no help given to the Catholic Irish. But these people were in the minority.

Certainly, the Reverend Valentine Pole Griffith did not believe this nor did his fellow Protestant George Frazer Brady who continued to send communications to Britain about men, women and children dying in Templecrone of hunger and disease, and asking for aid for them.

In a statement dated January 19, 1847, signed by Griffith and Brady, they described the absence of food, the mounting death toll, and the lack of public works and the continuing deterioration of the situation.[4]

"We feel astounded and dismayed at the accumulation of misery that presented itself to us; and we mourn as we persuade ourselves that such afflictions are but the shadows of things to come, and the beginning of unutterable sorrows."

On February 23rd, George Hancock, writing to the Society of Friends from onboard the steamer Albert, off Arranmore, described how he visited Arranmore and gave vouchers for oats to about 200 people who crowded around. All were sick with the fever and with dysentery.[5]

He stated that a modest Board of Works program had begun on the island repairing roads and that women and children, as young as 12, were trying to work because the men were either dead or too sick to leave their homes.

Among the scenes he witnessed were "a little boy who had just lost his father, and had his mother lying ill of fever, with no one to take care of the rest of the family; a poor girl unable to work any longer, who was struggling home."

As the tales of horror came out of Templecrone and were published in newspapers around Britain and Ireland, other investigators came and wrote about their own experiences. These stories tell of a relief committee being overwhelmed by a rising tide of famine and desolation and of the homes of Francis Forster and Reverend Valentine Griffith being continuously surrounded by scores of people crying for help.

There was little improvement by the 23rd of March when William Bennett of the Quakers visited Templecrone. He saw children eating seaweed in Arranmore and adults eating grass near Dungloe, and he lamented that all this could happen in the richest empire in the world.[6]

"The stubbornnest heart would break beneath the sight of the harmless multitude men, women, and little children pining away in want and misery our own fellow creatures and countrymen in this boasted land of wealth, civilization and humanity. And do, or do not, the causes and the responsibility lie with us?"

William Bennett was getting to the heart of the matter when he stood outside the rectory in Maghery on the evening of March 23rd, 1847, and lamented for the dying Irish, who he acknowledged as fellow countrymen, and yet who were being allowed to die by the British government even though Bennett believed that the cause of the catastrophe and the responsibility for it lay with the British Government.

Bennett, an Englishman, saw very clearly that if the government in London claimed jurisdiction over the Irish, then the government had a responsibility for their welfare. If the Irish were British citizens like Bennett, then why were they not being treated as the English would undoubtedly be treated in similar circumstances with assistance and compassion.

The reality of the matter was of course that Prime Minister Russell and his famine relief aid Trevelyn did not view the Irish as "real" British citizens: the Irish were in fact a conquered people who were ruled against their will and who could be treated outrageously because the British public really did not care very much how the Irish were treated.

When one of Prime Minister Russell's aides was told that a million Irish might die in the famine, he said that would not be nearly enough to do any good.

Other European governments when faced with hunger among their people went to the world marketplace and bought food to feed the hungry and the British could have done the same, had they wanted to.

The question that must be asked is if the famine had been taking place in the countryside outside London would it have been allowed to progress.

The answer, I believe, is no!

* * *

The widely held perception that all Irish landlords were bad landlords has little basis in reality. There were indeed bad landlords, but there were also good landlords, like Captain Conolly, the resident landlord in Lettermacaward.

Conolly worked hard both at home and in the Parliament to get aid into Donegal, and his tenants knew it and appreciated it.

Another erroneous perception is that Protestant clergymen used the destitution of Catholics to bribe them into abandoning their faith. A few Protestant clergymen were involved in this; the vast majority was not.

The Reverend Hart Molloy of Lettermacaward worked day and night to help all who lived in his parish and his efforts were appreciated by Catholics.

On February 28, 1847, the Catholics of the area publicly thanked the Reverend Molloy in a letter published in the *Londonderry Journal*.

"To the Editor of the *Londonderry Journal*
Lettermacaward, February 28, 1847

Sir:

I hope you will allow me in your journal to mention the praiseworthy exertions in the cause of the Reverend Hart Molloy, rector of this parish. The population is mostly Catholic, but this is no hindrance to his zeal. The whole year he has been visiting the poor day and night, traveling from house to house, and relieving their wants as far as he is able. Often has this venerable man, who is now seventy years of age, has been seen traveling from one end of the parish to the other, encountering rain, frost and snow, on his truly Christian mission. He even sold his crop of hay at a reduced price, to assist in keeping the souls and bodies of the sufferers together; and, but for him and Colonel Conolly, twenty would have fallen victim for one that did. Still, all their exertions would have been, in great measure, in vain, had they not been reinforced by Mr. Francis Forster and other gentlemen of the Rosses, who got meal shipped to Rutland Harbor [Burtonport] without which thousands would have perished, as provisions were completely exhausted in the district."[7]

The famine disease were rampant in Lettermacaward in the spring of 1847, and the Revered Molloy wrote to Dublin Castle on March 15th, advising the Central Relief Committee that he was secretary, treasurer and chairman because other officials were too ill to serve. He stated that the uncle of one official was the point of death.[8]

On March 20, Revered Molloy sent a letter to Routh with a list of donations that totaled 18 pounds and asking the "Irish government" to give "a like sum."[9]

Among the donors were: Colonel Conolly—23 pounds; the Society of Friends—78 pounds; Irish Relief Association—26 pounds; Belfast Ladies Association—20 pounds; the National Club—13 pounds; and the British Relief Association—20 pounds.

* * *

At the beginning of April, Conyngham's agent, Robert Russell, reneged on a public promise he had made at the mass meeting in Dungloe on August 10, 1846. At that meeting, attended by 2,000 of his tenants, Russell, on behalf of Conyngham, said that the tenants could eat their oats without fear, as he would see to it that they would have enough seed to plant the following year.

Then, with the oats gone, and all the livestock also dead, Russell told the tenants that Conyngham had not a shilling to give them.

In a complaint against Russell and Conyngham published in the *Londonderry Journal* on April 7, 1847, the "memorial from the inhabitants of Templecrone to His Excellency the Lord Lieutenant" stated that they had been ruined and deceived by the landlord and his agent.

"If we (who may survive until next year) perish for want of food, we have none to blame but the Marquis of Conyngham and his agent; our distress at present is extreme, many of us being obliged to subsist on one meal in two days—and the weakness of some such, that they cannot carry their dead to the proper place of burial—[instead] digging holes in the bog along the roadside. That our case requires peculiar remedies, it will be apparent to your Excellency, when we state that our landlord in this time of distress, has not done anything to alleviate our misery; and, were it not for the kind services of a few resident gentlemen, most of us would not be alive.

"Under these trying circumstances, we humbly solicit your Excellency to take our case into your kind consideration, and order a supply of food and seed to be sent us—and your Excellency's petitioners will ever pray."

The petition from Templecrone to the Lord Lieutenant illustrates a basic lack of understanding by the people of Templecrone of the predicament they were in.

Even at this late hour, these people did not seem to understand that Prime Minister Russell, Trevelyn, and the Lord Lieutenant were just not going to help them.

The people of Templecrone had absolute faith in the government—they believed that the government was not helping them because the government was not aware of the critical nature of the situation, and that if the government could only be informed of the true nature of Conyngham's failure to do his duty, then the government would surely step in and do the right thing.

This point of view had no basis in reality. The government was well aware of Conyngham's failure to help his tenants and well aware that they would die if some entity did not come to their aid.

But it was the government's intention that this entity was not going to be the government or its agents.

* * *

As the Irish crisis deepened, Prime Minister Russell's strategy was to publicly condemn the Irish landlords for failing to come to the aid of their tenants and to categorically deny that his government had any moral or legal obligation to provide the aid that the landlords could not or would not provide.

The *Times* of London supported Russell's position and there was a steady drumbeat of anti-landlord articles in the *Times* during 1846 and 1847.

Although British political leaders and the British media had been libeling Irish Catholics for centuries, the Anglo-Irish aristocracy did little to defend them, and not only that, the Anglo-Irish often went out of their way to join with the British in abusing Catholics.

However, when it appeared that the Anglo-Irish aristocracy was being blamed for Irish destitution and being driven to bankruptcy because of English laws that held them responsible for their tenants, the aristocracy began to fight back and to organize a united front to defend themselves against attacks from England.

On January 14, 1847, 600 of the leading Irish peers, landlords and members of Parliament met in the long room of the Rotunda, Dublin, to decide what they should do to protect themselves from the catastrophe that was rapidly overtaking them.

All 600 presented themselves as patriotic Irishmen who were being confronted by an implacable English enemy, although the only person who could really call himself an Irish patriot among those present was Daniel O'Connell, who was among the few Catholics in attendance.

Indeed, the majority of those present did not represent the middle class Protestant community either, never mind the ninety per cent of the population who were destitute Catholic. They were, in fact, an assembly of Earls, Lords, Marquis, Viscounts and Sirs who were representing themselves and nobody else. [10]

A review of the speeches presented, however, would have one believe that the famine had made Irish patriots out of all of them, because a motion to form an independent Irish party that would be formed out of those members who were presently Torys and Whigs was carried unanimously.

Other motions were carried that day also—motions that had been proposed previously but ignored by most of those present.

There was a motion carried that held the state responsible for feeding the Irish; a motion was carried to demand that the government bring in food in navy ships and make it available to the starving; a motion was carried to scrap the present Board of Works system and institute a new system that would pay people to improve their lands and to build an infrastructure of railroads and piers that would be an aid to commerce.

All of these motions were carried without dissent and with a great deal of enthusiasm, and when Viscount Milton got up and proposed that the British government should provide financial assistance to all the destitute who wanted to emigrate, this motion, too, was carried by all present, including O'Connell, and his son, John.

Sub-committees were then formed, and each sub-committee fleshed out the motions into detailed proposals, and these proposals were then presented to the leaders of Ireland at the same time that they were presented to Lord John Russell.

The proposal for government assisted emigration, however, had somehow evolved into a greatly expanded plan entitled the Irish Colonization Plan, and the core of this plan was to have the British government spend 9 million pounds transporting 1,500,000 destitute Irish to Canada, where they would be encouraged to till the land and colonize new areas. John O'Connell's signature was on a copy of a plan sent to the Right Reverend Dr. Maginn, Bishop of Derry, with a cover letter asking him to lend his support to the proposal.

Dr. Maginn was furious at the proposal and antagonistic to O'Connell for going along with it. Dr. Maginn believed that John O'Connell had disgraced his illustrious father Daniel O'Connell by supporting the plan—apparently not being aware that Daniel O'Connell was also in the Rotunda when a less complex plan had been proposed and he had agreed to it.

Maginn wrote back to the Irish Party lashing it with contempt.

"Why have the barefaced impudence to ask me to consent to the expatriation of millions of my co-religionists and fellow countrymen. You, the hereditary oppressors of my race and my religion—you, who reduced one of the noblest people under heaven who live on the most fertile island on earth, to the worst species of a miserable exotic [the potato] which no humane man having anything better would constantly give to his swine or his horses—you, who have made the most beautiful island under the sun a land of skulls or of ghastly specters—you are anxious, I presume, to get a Catholic bishop to abet your wholesale system of extermination—to head in pontificals the convoy of your exiles, and thereby give the sanction of religion to your atrocious scheme."

The bishop then went on to propose to the British government that instead of dumping millions of destitute tenants on Canadian shores that the government dump all those responsible for the situation, including landlords, government officials, peers, and the leaders of British political parties, in Canada instead.

Finally, he stated that he would have nothing to do with the plan because he recognized the names of most of those who signed the proposals as being the descendants of Cromwellian conquerors who had stolen the land from the native Irish and had been abusing them since then.

This particular colonization plan was badly received throughout Ireland, and Lord Russell quietly backed away from it, saying that natural emigration would probably take care of the problem at no cost to the government. He was right: the Irish fled Ireland by the millions in the decades after the famine, and the total was many times the mere 1.5 million proposed in 1847 by the landlords.

But Russell would have nothing to do with a proposal Bishop Maginn had included in his reply to supporters of the colonization plan: namely to give all the vast stretches of unused land in Ireland to those 1.5 million and spend the 9 million pounds developing it into arable land. Maginn asked, why send people to Canada to develop waste land, when they could do the same in their own country?

The Marquis of Conyngham was wholeheartedly in agreement with Russell's rejection of the Maginn proposal. Sixty percent of his estate in Templecrone was undeveloped bog that could be drained and turned into farmland. But he would not drain it; would not give it to some of the landless serfs to drain; and would rather ship 80% of his tenants to Canada—if someone else paid the voyage—than take any steps to improve their lot at home.

* * *

However, the Irish landlords who were determined to get rid of the tenants who had become a financial burden on them did not give up when their attempts to ship 1.5 million indigent Irish abroad met with rejection.

When new legislation was put through the British Parliament in April of 1847 allowing the funding of soup kitchens for those who were destitute William Henry Gregory, an M.P. from Dublin, inserted two clauses in the bill—which was entitled "The Poor Relief (Ireland) Bill"—which he succeeded in getting passed.

One clause stated that any tenant with a rated value of less than five pounds who gave up his land to his landlord could receive assisted emigration from both the landlord and the local board of guardians.

This was optional, of course, and some who were alienated from conditions in Ireland welcomed it.

However, the second clause mandated that no tenant who had more than a quarter acre of land could receive food from the soup kitchens, unless the tenant agreed to give back his land to the landlord. Thus, 95% of the tenants in places like Templecrone, had to make themselves homeless or they would get no food.

The Gregory clause was, in fact, a tool of the landlords to force tenants off the land under threat of starvation and then get them out of the country altogether by offering to pay their way abroad.

This was the colonization plan again, presented this time in new clothing, and it worked, because tenants began to leave the Irish countryside in droves.

Further pressure was put on the destitute by shutting down the Board of Works projects in June. The British government gave as a reason for this the fact that soup kitchens for the destitute were now in operation and they did not need the money from working to get food, since they were getting food from the soup kitchens.

But if the small tenants had been earning money for food on the Board of Works they would not have needed to go to the soup kitchens for food, and if they did not need the soup kitchens they would not have to abandon their farms for food or emigrate to survive. So, the closing down of the Board of Works was one more strategy to separate the poor Irish from their land and drive them into exile. In many instances it worked.

The closing of the Board of Works projects did not have much impact in Templecrone, since the last authorization in January—worth about 7,000 pounds—which was made available had already been exhausted. Much of it had been spent in make-work projects, like roads to nowhere.

Meanwhile, the wily Celts of Templecrone found a way around the infamous Gregory clause which Conyngham had hoped would clear his estate of the indigent.

The language of the clause read that a head of the household, and those supported by the head could not get relief if he held more than a quarter acre, and to get around this the head of households were subletting all of their land except one eighth of an acre around the dwelling to the oldest unmarried son, who then threw up a shack and told the landlord he was not applying for relief—it was only his parents and siblings who were living on the one eighth acre who were destitute and needed help.

Conyngham was furious at this ploy, but he was afraid to challenge his tenants since landlords who evicted destitute tenants were being murdered in other areas, and Conyngham was not a brave man, in spite of all his military titles.

So, in 1847, in spite of all efforts to dislodge them, the Celts of Templecrone clung to their bogs, glens and mountains, refusing to emigrate, and preferring to die of hunger or disease in the only homeland they or their ancestors had ever known.

CHAPTER ELEVEN

The rampant disease and death in Templecrone created two occupations that had not existed before the famine.

One, was that of an independent contractor who was authorized to pick up dead bodies lying in the bogs and fields and carry them to the graveyard for burial; the other was the fever nurse who nursed the dying for a fee.

The unusual thing about these nurses was that the majority of them never got sick themselves—they seemed to be immune to the diseases that killed others.

The folklore from the famine era is full of stories about the corpse contractors and the nurses. Even 100 years after the famine, people talked in whispers about the men who gathered up the dead, and the women who nursed the dying. The storytellers seemed to believe there was something unnatural or supernatural about the activities of both types of occupations.

Many believed that it was desperation that drove men to agree to pick up dead bodies in exchange for a fee. It was believed these men had no other means of support, and the fee earned enabled them to survive for a few more days or even a week.

A type of body bag made of sally rods or straw was developed and the body was carried on the back of the contractor and deposited in a mass grave. Bodies were piled on top of one another and lightly covered with dirt and the next body was thrown in on top of the previous one.

Sometimes a body had to be carried for miles, and if the body was already beginning to decompose, then the chore of getting it to a grave could be a very unpleasant one indeed.

The bodies of children were much easier to handle, especially the very young. According to the Protestant community living in Carnbuoy, a nearby island named Oilean Na Marbh—the island of the dead—was used as a mass grave for children and 500 were buried there during the famine, and many of these children were carried there by the contractor, because their parents were already dead or were too weak to carry the bodies themselves. In some instances during 1847, the parents died first, leaving a number of small children behind, and then these children died, one by one, often with no one to take care of them in their final hours.

The contractors who survived the famine found themselves isolated from the rest of the community, either because of fear of them, or because other survivors despised them for what they did to survive.

Arguments like—"somebody had to do this terrible job"—rarely were understood or appreciated.

The fever nurses inspired an entirely different reaction—they were looked upon with awe, as if surviving while others died was some kind of personal achievement, in fact a triumph.

As the fever epidemic progressed, these women were hired as soon as the typhus made its appearance in the house, while the rest of the family moved out to a make-shift dwelling some distance from the house.

The nurse then stayed with the patients until they recovered—or died.

A fever hospital was opened in Dungloe in 1847 and one was also opened in Burtonport.

J.F. O'Donnell, who was 81 years of age in 1945 and who lived in Burtonport, told a collector from the Folklore Commission that when he was very young he had been told by old people that the hospital opened in Burtonport had been converted from a warehouse owned by Conyngham.

"It was a three story building with a good roof of slate. Every one of the three floors was full of fever victims."

J.F. said a relative of his was hired as one of the fever nurses and was given a half a crown a week to tend to the sick. He said she never got sick herself.

Behind the hospital was a mass grave where fever fatalities were buried.

* * *

Nora Green from Arranmore, my great grand aunt, was another of these women who took care of the sick, but never got sick herself.

Nora was a noted herbalist, who acted both as doctor and nurse and who had a whole range of medicines that she concocted from the wild herbs which grew on Arranmore.

Long before the famine, people came from far and wide to be treated by Nora—even coming in from the mainland.

Nora could do little for the victims of the epidemic of typhus and dysentery that swept across Arranmore, but she did her best. She had no hesitation in going into a house with fever victims in it, even though she knew the disease was contagious, and she weathered the famine without ever getting infected.

Nora handed down her skills as an herbalist to my grandfather, Timothy Gallagher, who used to treat people in Inishfree.

Tim had a whole shelf-full of medicine bottles in his pantry, and this medicine was used to treat all kinds of ailments.

Tim would never give the recipe for his medicines to anyone, however, and his pharmaceutical secrets died with him in 1956.

* * *

The fever epidemic wrecked the Gaelic social system that had been in place in Templecrone before the famine. Friendship, or the reaching out to relatives, became a thing of the past.

"The famine ruined everything," said Maire Ni Greinne of Ranafast. "Your only friend was the person who gave you food."

In 1847 there was no sharing of resources anymore—because resources were very limited. People who helped others were the exception, not the rule.

James O'Donnell, 87, of Ranafast, said in 1945 that his father had told him that when a soup caldron was set up in the area there were wild scenes when the soup was being distributed.

"Everybody was trampling over each other, trying to get the soup. Once a woman fainted trying to get to the cauldron. She was carried out from the crowd by two men and left there. One man took the place of the woman, and was grabbed by the back of the neck and pulled away."[2]

O'Donnell's father was one of seven children, and he and a sister were the only ones to survive the fever. The other five died, one by one.

The old custom of welcoming everyone who came to the door died with the fever epidemic, because people were afraid that a stranger would bring disease to the house.

My father's grandfather, Daniel Sweeney, had always been proud of his hospitality, but he, too, would not allow a stranger in his house, and if a beggar knocked at his door, he would give the beggar an alm, but never let the beggar in.

All social life ground to a halt as the epidemic progressed. People who used to congregate together to dance or to sing no longer did so, and even the custom of visiting neighbors to tell stories by the fireside came to an end. Everybody huddled in their own homes and prayed to survive.

* * *

Because of the total destitution in Templecrone, most of the people in the area did not have seed potatoes to set in the spring of 1847, and only for the efforts of the Relief Committee to acquire seed, none would have been planted at all.

The Templecrone Relief Committee had begged for seed from the government, from the Quakers, and from the British Association, and as a result of these efforts a great deal of seed was planted, but the crops were only 50% of the crops of pre-famine years.

An effort was made to import seeds from countries not hit by the blight in 1845 and 1846, but nevertheless people were apprehensive that the crop would fail for the third time in a row.

In Arranmore, my great grandparents, Bryan and Maura Gallagher went out into the potato fields as soon as the stalks began to bloom and every day they knelt in the soft soil and prayed that the potatoes would stay healthy. Other families in Balintra said the rosary every night for the success of the potato crop.

Near Dungloe, my father's grandparents, James and Mary Campbell kept an eye on the potato crop all day, every day, but there are no family legends about prayer vigils on the Campbell potato fields.

As June progressed and the potatoes seemed to be thriving, there was a great temptation to dig into the soil and sample the potatoes—and many succumbed to the temptation and dug the potatoes up. They turned out to be large and healthy.

During the middle of June, the early crop of potatoes were dug up all over the parish and found to be healthy, and those families who had not tasted potatoes in two years consumed vast quantities, as if afraid the potatoes would rot before they could be eaten.

The potato crop of 1847 did not solve food shortages in Templecrone—all it did was to buy some time for the people. The crop was not nearly big enough to feed all the people for the entire year, so starvation still was on the horizon and supplementary rations were still needed.

The Quakers granted Francis Forster five major shipments of food in the summer of 1847, all handed over by Forster to the Templecrone Relief Committee, who in turn made soup from these supplies.[3]

On June 9th, Forster received two tons of Indian meal and two tons of rice; on June 19th, he received four tons of Indian meal, two tons of rice, 10 sacks of peas, and almost a ton of wheaten meal; on July 10th he received three tons of Indian meal, five sacks of peas, one ton of rice, and a ton of biscuits. On July 21st, he received another ton of biscuits; and on July 24th, he was given the loan of 200 pounds to invest in the kelp industry.

Once again, the Quakers were out in front, insuring that the havoc created by starvation was lessened, and the British Association worked hand in hand with the Quakers, focusing on the health of the children, in an effort to ensure that another generation would grow up in the parish.

But even an abundance of food could not curb the death march of disease across the parish, which seemed to grow worse as a wide variety of illnesses joined the forces of typhus and dysentery which were the leading causes of death.

The fever hospital in Dungloe was full as soon as it opened, and even a high death rate could not provide vacancies for all who wanted to get in.

According to local folklore, whole families left Dun No Mainsear, near Annagary, and headed for the poorhouse in Glenties, where they met with rejection and were forced to lie outside and wait for admission. Many died waiting.

In Annagary dead bodies were found in drains, who were either abandoned there by their families, or were fever victims who had been trying to find shelter.

In Comeen, four brothers died one after another of fever and were buried beside their house. The house was burned down by neighbors after the last one died.

There were instances when a family split up after one member came down with the fever, with the sick member being abandoned by other members of the family who were afraid that if they stayed they too would be infected.

* * *

At the end of March 1847, the Reverend Hart Molloy of Lettermacaward wrote a letter to Dublin Castle pleading for help because there were no provisions in the area and warning that if sufficient help did not come soon that violence would break out and that the people would begin "stealing for the belly."[4]

Two months later, on the 2nd of June, Molloy's prophecy came true, when a ship laden with wheaten meal was surrounded by three boats from Arranmore and almost three tons of meal was stolen from the ship. The ship was the "Larne" which had set sail from Belfast and was on her way to Sligo.[5]

As usual, such an incident created an uproar in official circles and there was an immediate investigation launched by the coast guard and the police to catch these perpetrators of this "diabolical act of piracy."

Arranmore was invaded by a search party armed with information given by an informer and 12 bags of meal were recovered—out of the 26 stolen—and three men were taken prisoner but 19 others, who had been named, escaped because they had been warned, and were not in their homes when the search party arrived.

Two of the arrested men, the Boyle brothers, turned state's evidence and spent the next several years in jail waiting for the trial to come up, while their families fled Arranmore and went to Scotland. In Scotland the families were supported by the British government.

Once again the British put vast resources into trying to apprehend those who escaped, as if they had committed some heinous crime that could neither be overlooked nor excused and some of these men, who were on the run, never returned home again but lived their lives in exile in Britain, Australia and the United States.

Those who raided the Larne were not considered pirates by the people of Templecrone and their escapade was not viewed as criminal in nature by local people. These men had decided that their families and their neighbors were starving and they believed that the situation justified the action taken.

The only regrets anyone had were that informers had named the men involved, thereby putting the lives of the men and those of their families in jeopardy.

The informers were despised as traitors, and were viewed as criminals who had violated the social code of the community.

No voice in Templecrone was raised to condemn the "pirates" and no voice was raised either to support those who turned them in.

The priests and Protestant ministers were silent on the issue, and so was Forster, although he was alleged to have said afterwards that such actions, given the situation, were predictable.

Forster was, of course, correct—it should have come as no surprise that a desperate people would try to steal in order to survive, and the only surprise that came out of Templecrone in the famine years was that there was not a lot more violence than there was.

* * *

While the people of Templecrone died in their hovels and were buried in their back gardens, Her Royal Highness Queen Victoria gave a state ball on Friday, May 13, 1847, which was attended by more than a thousand of the aristocracy of Britain and Ireland.

The *Times* gave the ball a wonderful review and described in detail the luxury of it all. Magnificent cut glass and gold chandeliers illuminated the ballrooms at Buckingham Palace and "plants of the greatest beauty and rarity were arranged in the recesses of the different saloons."[6]

The ladies who attended the event were dressed in exotic costumes "composed of the richest and most costly fabrics in silk and satin of the most elegant design. The dresses were most splendidly ornamented with diamonds, pearls and precious stones."

The Queen wore a "magnificent" dress, and a head-dress encrusted with diamonds. Prince Albert wore a field marshal's uniform and he displayed the stars of the Order of St. Patrick. Supper was served at midnight, on gold plate. Wine was served in goblets glittering with precious stones. Salmon, veal, pheasant, shrimp and sides of beef, lamb, and venison were laid out on gold platters whose rims were studded with gems.

An army of waiters in dress uniform served the thousand guests, and another army of servants brought the food from the kitchens to the ballroom.

As the evening progressed, the Lord Chamberlain, by Her Majesty's command, formed a quadrille, and Prince Albert led all the distinguished guests in dancing.

The royal gala went on into the small hours of the morning, and, when it was over, the guests trooped out of the gates of Buckingham Palace, where a vast array of elegant coaches with uniformed lackeys waited to ferry them home to their mansions, townhouses, and palaces.

It was an evening when England put on display her vast wealth and her affluent aristocracy, and although the *Times* mentioned only a few of the aristocrats who were present there is little doubt that the Marquis of Conyngham and his wife were present, as attendance at a state ball was a command performance and this was one event that the Conynghams just had to be seen at, regardless of the condition of their tenants in Templecrone.

CHAPTER TWELVE

As the destitution deepened in the fall of 1847, the British became even more determined that the Irish be made responsible for their own salvation and that the British treasury be protected from demands made on it to feed the starving Irish.

Lord Clarendon, the Lord Lieutenant, sent a communication to Prime Minister Russell urging immediate government aid, but Russell rejected him.

Clarendon was very well aware of the prejudice that existed in England against helping the Irish, but he believed it was unthinkable to leave the Irish to their own resources, because the resources to solve the problem were just not there.

"We are not to let the people die of starvation," Clarendon wrote. "We must not believe that rebellion is impossible."

Russell replied, "The state of Ireland for the next few months must be one of great suffering. Unhappily the agitation for repeal has continued to destroy nearly all sympathy in this country."[1]

The agitation for "repeal" that Russell was referring to was the decade old campaign to repeal the Act of Union with Britain, and reopen the Irish Parliament which had been abolished when the two countries were united in a shotgun marriage after the rebellion of 1798.

This was not a campaign for total independence from Britain—just a campaign to restore local government; but even this limited objective had infuriated the British government, which viewed it as the treacherous act of an ungrateful people who had no thanks for all Britain had done for them.

Of course the Irish believed that no thanks were due because, from their point of view, the English had subjugated the Irish, stolen its resources, and were now deliberately withholding aid from a dying nation.

The British now enacted laws that, when enforced, taxed every area with additional taxes called rates that were designed to make every landlord and every small farmer bear the full brunt of famine relief. For instance, the taxes on Templecrone were astronomically high—far above the ability of anyone to pay even at the best of times—and if these taxes were not collected, then the local headquarters of the relief committees in Glenties had no way of financing the poorhouse or the soup kitchens, if the Quakers or the British Association and other groups did not help.

And no matter how much Clarendon or relief officials insisted that the money was not in places like Templecrone and therefore no taxes could be collected, Russell and his Chancellor of the Exchequer, Sir Charles Wood, would still reject this argument.

"The principle of the Poor Law as you very well know is that rate after rate should be levied for the purpose of preserving life until the landlord and the farmer either enable the people to support themselves by honest industry or dispose of their estates to those who can perform these indispensable duties."

And when Clarendon replied that there were landlords who were unable or unwilling to pay, there was an answer for that too.

"Arrest, remand, do anything you can. Send horse, foot and dragoons, all the world will applaud you, and I shall not at all be squeamish as to what I did, to the verge of the law, and a little beyond."[2]

This type of response could only be considered a rational response as far as Templecrone was concerned if there were wealthy families and landlords who were well able to pay their taxes and were not doing so, or were able to create jobs on their estates for their tenants and were not doing that either.

But Conyngham, according to himself, was deeply in debt, and therefore supposedly could do nothing, and the only other farmer of note was Forster, and he appeared to be doing all he could, and as for the rest of the occupiers of land in the area, they were all lined up at soup kitchens, begging for food.

What point, then, was there to go on demanding that the taxes be collected or advocating an invasion of cavalry? Could the troops bring blood out of a stone?

Anyway, Lord Russell could have apprehended most of the offending landlords anytime he wanted—most of them, including Conyngham had town houses in London, and he met them frequently at clubs and the social functions thrown by the aristocracy.

But the landlords had little to fear from Russell's tough stand against aid for the Irish, as they did not face death by starvation. It was the people living in the remote hills and glens who were in mortal danger from Russell's policies. It was they who paid with their lives for his unwillingness to help.

* * *

Francis Forster was totally opposed to the policies of the British government, and for good reason. He believed he was a good landlord who was doing all he could to help his tenants, but he was being punished for the actions of Conyngham, a bad landlord, who was doing nothing.

When Conyngham refused to pay his share of the rates, the whole burden fell on Forster and he knew he was just not able to carry the burden.

Conyngham not only let Forster bear all the risks and all the costs of relief, he took advantage of the fact that Forster was also feeding his tenants and he ordered Robert Russell to seize all the tenant assets he could lay hands on in lieu of rent. Russell and his bailiffs roamed Templecrone in the fall of 1847 and gathered up all the potatoes, oats and turnips they could, frightening the tenants into giving up their food under the threat of eviction.

This callous and barbaric act was Russell's last hurrah in Templecrone, because shortly afterwards, in October, he was promoted to the post of agent for all of Conyngham's Donegal property and took up residence in the south of the county.

Conyngham was obviously rewarding Russell for his zeal in robbing the destitute tenants, but Russell's move out of Templecrone was a move also designed to save his life because some of the tenants had become so hostile to him that he could have been assassinated had he remained on in the parish.

Forster himself was very concerned about the ugly mood that had been growing in the parish, because on September 19th he asked that troops be stationed in the area to protect government officials and government property.

Forster wrote to the Lord Lieutenant in his capacity as resident magistrate about his fears that law and order could not be maintained.[3]

"I think it is my duty to state for the information of the Lord Lieutenant ... though the people have been very quiet considering the awful state of destitution they were, and are in, on this coast, yet we cannot venture to say they will continue quiet—when it is in fact well known that all the crops grown this year in this district will not feed the people four months."

Forster went on to state that all the cattle had been sold, there was no employment and no money to buy food. So, as a precaution, troops should be stationed at Meenmore Barracks. If troops were not stationed in Templecrone, then it was probable that the ships coming into Burtonport with provisions would be attacked the way the Lame was attacked earlier.

* * *

Conyngham's failure to pull his weight continued to infuriate Forster and he decided to get revenge by once again putting the spotlight on the condition of Conyngham's tenants.

Forster's strategy was to invite a prominent American author of religious books, Anseth Nicholson, to Templecrone to witness first-hand the destitution of the parish.

Nicholson was a Christian fundamentalist who had written a book about bringing bible studies to Irish Catholics, and her book had made her widely known in Britain.

In bringing in Nicholson, Forster used the same strategy he had used so effectively with the *Times* reporter in September of 1845: he brought the author to Arranmore, the most destitute area in Templecrone, and let her see the destitution at its worst.

Nicholson was horrified at what she saw—mass graves with bodies barely covered with soil; dogs sleek and well fed from eating corpses in the graveyard; and a population of walking skeletons. According to Reverend Valentine Griffith, hundreds had already died in Arranmore, and Nicholson later wrote in *Lights and Shades of Ireland*, published in 1851, that Griffith had written to her in the spring of 1849 that the death toll had risen to 500 at that time.[4]

After her visit to Arranmore, which had traumatized her, Griffith brought her to his rectory at Maghery, where she met Mrs. Griffith who told her that every night bodies were left outside their door by people too weak and too poor to give a Christian burial to their relatives. These people knew that if they left the bodies at the rector's door the deceased would get a decent burial.

After her visit to Templecrone Nicholson decided to pay a visit to the Hill estate in Gweedore to see first-hand an estate that had the reputation of being well-managed . Her visit had not been planned by Forster, but he could not very well refuse to take her there.

Forster had been able to manipulate Thomas Campbell Foster, the *Times* reporter, back in 1845, and get him to write a glowing report about the Hill estate, but there was no possibility of manipulating Nicholson, because Nicholson would describe what she witnessed anyway.

Nicholson stayed in Hill's hotel in Gweedore and was horrified at the hundreds of people outside the inn begging for food and clothing. Nicholson met a Mrs. Hewitson, a representative of the Belfast Ladies Association at the inn, and Mrs. Hewitson said that most of those outside begging would be dead in a month.

Obviously, conditions on the Hill estate were no better than those on the Conyngham estate, and Nicholson stated this in her report on conditions in Donegal.

Francis Forster succeeded in embarrassing Conyngham by turning Nicholson loose in Templecrone, and her eye-witness report created a great deal of bad publicity for him in England. But Forster did not succeed in getting him to pull his weight in Templecrone. He still would not get involved in famine relief.

* * *

Although Conyngham and his agents mistreated their tenants in 1847, there were other landlords in Ireland who were much more callous to their tenants than he was.

A landlord named Walsh evicted three whole villages in Belmullet in December of 1847 and drove men, women and children out into the snow, with the help of the 49th Regiment.[5]

The evicted people tried to find shelter that night in makeshift huts on the landlord's bogs, but Walsh was back the next day, and with the help of the British troops drove them off the bogs.

The Quakers and the British Association came to the aid of the evicted with food and clothing, and the evicted families retreated into the mountains where they built hovels made of sod and branches of trees. Walsh wanted the troops to evict the families from the mountains, but the troops refused, and the families stayed in that area, living like animals in the wild.

Incidents such as this were repeated all over Ireland in 1847 and 1848, with hundreds of thousands of people driven off the land by landlords who did not want to pay the taxes to support them. A man named Higgins, who was a British Association volunteer, told James Tuke, the Quaker, that he wished he had the authority to shoot Walsh.

Further south, a Captain Arthur Kennedy, a British Army officer involved in evictions in Clare, recalled these evictions later on in life and said that he was tempted many times to take his gun and shoot some of the landlords he had met.

* * *

The idea of shooting landlords also occurred to the evicted tenants, and some landlords were indeed murdered, although the numbers were not great.

The most publicized of these murders was the shooting of Major Mahon, a landlord who evicted 3,006 persons from his Roscommon estate.

Mahon had chartered two ships to take some of the evicted to Canada, and a number of the tenants died on the voyage across the Atlantic.

The shooting of Mahon, on November 2, 1847, was an act of revenge by relatives of the deceased.

Mahon's murder created an uproar in the media in both Britain and Ireland. No sympathy was expressed by British officials for the dead tenants whose bodies were thrown overboard on the Atlantic voyage, but the landlord's murder was viewed by the establishment as a major crime against the state and no expense was spared to find the killers.

Eventually, two men were executed for the murder.

In all, a total of 16 landlords were murdered in 1847, all of them killed in retaliation for evicting tenants. Six of these were major landlords; the other 10 were either agents or small land owners who were, like Forster, not categorized as aristocracy from an old family.

The only positive thing that can be said about Conyngham is that he did not get involved in mass evictions. He may have done nothing to help his tenants, but he did not dump them on the roadside in the middle of winter either, and for this reason he does not belong in the very worst category of landlords.

Landlords all over Ireland were panic-stricken by the attacks and they hired bodyguards to protect themselves.

Conyngham's principle agent, Sir John Benbow, did not go on his annual trip to Templecrone because he thought it unwise to do so.

It was during this period that Robert Russell persuaded Benbow and Conyngham to transfer him to south Donegal and allow him to monitor the Templecrone estate from a distance. Conyngham understood his apprehension and let him move. Charles Sproule, a Burtonport merchant, was appointed sub-agent to Russell.[7]

There was a hue and cry among the landlord class to enact new laws to deal with the rising violence.

Clarendon saw in the murders a conspiracy that was designed to drive all of the landlords out of Ireland and allow the tenants to take possession. He was convinced another Irish rebellion was in its early stages.

Among the laws that Clarendon suggested was a law that would make all people in any area where a murder was committed responsible for the crime unless the residents informed on the perpetrators. He also wanted all firearms banned, and he wanted penal servitude for anyone caught out at night in disguise.

Lord Russell, who cared as little for Irish landlords as he did for their tenants, said there should be laws enacted against the behavior of the landlords also. He said English landlords did not throw their tenants out on the roadside in the middle of winter and then burn their houses down.

However, punitive laws were passed in December of 1847, but they had little impact because they were neither practical nor enforceable.

Many landlords who had resided on their estates fled and never came back again. Those who stayed carried firearms and many had bodyguards.

Captain Pole, who worked for the Treasury Department, told Routh that the landlords were isolated from their tenants and were surrounded by a hostile population.

Even Francis Forster who had made a major contribution to famine relief went around armed and had two bailiffs as bodyguards. He said that in 1847 he felt like an outcast in his own country, among a population who no longer quite accepted him as one of their own.

* * *

Forster may have had grounds for complaint in 1847, because during the latter half of 1845 and all through 1846 and 1847 he had been a responsible resident landlord who had worked tirelessly to feed the hungry and there is no doubt he saved hundreds, if not thousands of lives by his efforts.

But in December of 1847, Forster became involved in a business deal that involved the purchase of Arranmore Island by his son-in-law Walter Chorley from Conyngham at a bargain price and the results of that deal had fatal consequences for dozens of the islanders.

Conyngham had wanted to sell Arranmore because the island had become a major psychological burden after the *Times* expose of 1845.

When Anseth Nicholson put the spotlight on Aranmore again in 1847, Conyngham was eager to get rid of the island at any price.

Enter Walter Chorley with an offer to buy the island for 200 pounds—an offer that never would have been accepted prior to 1845, but which was now accepted eagerly by the beleaguered Conyngham.

Chorley had plans for the island and these were the same plans his father-in-law had helped Lord George Hill put into effect when Hill took over the Gweedore estate.

Chorley's plan was to evict all those sub-tenants who were not paying rent directly to Conyngham and to consolidate small holdings into bigger holdings, which would make the holdings more valuable and this would enable him to increase the rent threefold.[8]

His plan also called for him to clear a major section of the Leabgarrow area of Arranmore and operate a large farm there himself, and to take personal possession of mountain areas, until then used as a common area, and graze his own sheep and cattle there.

Chorley believed he could have his investment back in two years, and then he could enjoy rents three times the amount Conyngham was getting, and still operate a large farm himself.

Chorley realized, of course, that he was gambling on being able to solve a number of problems before Arranmore would generate a great deal of income for him.

His first gamble was that the 1848 potato crop would be a healthy one, which would enable his surviving tenants to begin paying the high rents immediately.

The second problem was that it was imperative that he would not be liable for the taxes to support his evicted tenants, because these taxes would eliminate all his income from the increased rents.

In order to avoid responsibility for the evicted tenants, Chorley had to get them out of the electoral division that Arranmore was part of, and then he would no longer be held responsible for them, since taxpayers were only responsible for those who lived in their own electoral division.

Arranmore was part of the electoral division that comprised Burtonport, Dungloe and half of southern Templecrone. Northern Templecrone was part of the Mullaghderg electoral division.

If Chorley dumped all of his evicted tenants on the mainland at Burtonport or Dungloe he would still be responsible for them since these areas were still in his electoral division.

If he dumped the tenants in the Mullaghderg electoral division, he would hurt his father-in-law, who owned a great deal of land there.

So, he had to come up with a solution that would rid him of these troublesome paupers without creating problems for Francis Forster.

His solution was an ingenious one, which solved the problem but was a case study in cruelty, deception and total indifference to any code of honor. And the solution involved the collusion of Chorley, Forster, Conyngham and his agent Russell and the chairman of the Relief Commission in Glenties, Captain William O'Neill.

Charley's solution was to have Arranmore declared a separate electoral division from either North or South Templecrone. Approval for this would have to be given by the Poor Law Commissioners of Northwest Donegal.

After Chorley had received this new status for Arranmore, he planned to evict all the targeted tenants and dump them on the mainland, which would be an entirely separate electoral division by this time.

Since they were no longer in the Arranmore electoral division, Chorley would not be held responsible for aiding them, and since they had not been residents of either the north or south Templecrone divisions, Forster would not be held responsible for them either, and the tenants would have no option but to head out of Templecrone altogether to the poorhouse in Glenties, which was the only facility that could provide some assistance to them.

The first public indication that Arranmore might change hands was on December 10, 1847, when Conyngham's agent petitioned the Poor Law Guardians to change the electoral status of Arranmore.[9]

The letter from Russell was to Captain O'Neill, chairman of the Relief Commissioners in Glenties.

"A capitalist has offered to purchase the island of Arranmore, in Glenties Union, and proposes to employ all the population there, provided it can be formed into an electoral division of itself.

"I need not state to you, who know the condition of the islanders and the burden they are on the electoral division of which the island forms a part, all parties are concerned that this arrangement should be made; and by your representing it in the proper light to the Poor Law Commissioners, have no doubt that the request will be granted."

Captain O'Neill presented Russell's request to the Poor Law Commissioners with a cover letter.

"I have the honour to submit, for your consideration, a letter from Mr. Russell, agent to the Marquis of Conyngham, relative to the island of Arranmore, requesting that the island be made into an electoral division on to itself.

"This is a course I would strongly recommend, as it is the most miserable and wretched part of the electoral division it belongs to, and of the whole Union, and is at present a heavy burden on both.

"The case is evidently different from any application of the kind that has hitherto been made to the Commissioners.

"I understand that Mr. Chorley, of Belfast, who is the person he alludes to, intends building a house and residing on the island, and exerting himself in every way to improve the condition of the people."

The Poor Law Commissioners studied the proposal for more than a week, and then rejected it on January 3, 1848.

The rejection of the Chorley plan was probably based on the total lack of credibility the plan had with those who reviewed it.

There is no doubt Chorley was viewed as a speculator and the Commissioners would not have to be prophets to predict what would happen if they gave Chorley the approval he wanted.

But Chorley was determined to have Arranmore and turn it into a highly profitable estate, and when he failed to get the approval for a new electoral division, he unveiled his backup plan, which was even more dishonorable than the first one.

Chorley's backup plan was to charter a ship, which he berthed at Donegal Town, 35 miles from Arranmore, and then to evict the tenants and tell them that if they made their way to Donegal Town the ship would take them, free of charge, to Canada.

Chorley put this plan into effect when he officially took over the island in January of 1848. His first action was to review Conyngham's rent records to see who among the tenants had paid rent directly to Conyngham and who had not.

Any tenant who had sublet land from another tenant and was not on Conyngham's rent roll was given an eviction notice and was ordered off the island by March 1, 1848. No evicted family would be permitted to find shelter with a relative—they had to leave the island voluntarily or they would be deported by force.

All were offered the option of emigrating, and if they turned this down, they would have to find shelter in the poorhouse in Glenties.

Chorley refused to allow those who were terminally ill from fever to remain on the island, and he showed no compassion to widows who had droves of dependent children. All had to leave.

On March 1st, Chorley was on hand to see to it that all of the evicted tenants left the island, and those who did not have someone to ferry them to the mainland were ferried on boats hired by Chorley.[10]

There were heart-rending scenes at the pier as the evicted tenants left the island and journeyed off into an unknown future.

Aranmore had been the only home most of them had ever known and the ties to the island went back for hundreds of years.

Many of those departing were afraid they would not survive the ocean voyage to America and their apprehension was not without foundation. The *Londonderry Journal* carried stories all through 1846 and 1847 of emigrant ships which had left Northwest Ireland and were lost at sea, and other stories were published about huge numbers of fatalities at sea, as passengers died of fever and their bodies were thrown overboard.

Above all, there was a terror of the unknown: there had been little emigration from Arranmore prior to the famine, and these sick and destitute families had no relatives in America to welcome them or to inform them about what to expect—if they ever got there.

But those who intended to go to America and those people who were allowed to remain in Arranmore knew this parting was permanent and that the chances that the emigrants would ever see Arranmore again were very slim indeed. This made the occasion very emotional.

The hundreds of evicted tenants were deposited on the mainland at an area near Burtonport and told it was their responsibility to find their way over the mountains to Donegal Town.

Some of the families left the main group and made their way to relatives living on the mainland on the Conyngham estate and begged for shelter. These people, some of whom were very sick, would rather die at home than die on the way to Donegal Town or on the boat to America. They were taken in by relatives and they never left Templecrone.

The weather was damp and bitterly cold as the remainder began the long trek and by the time the group had crossed the Gweebarra River and into Glenties it was nightfall and they were too exhausted to continue.

Not all of the group arrived in Glenties—many could not keep up with the main group and fell behind and were not seen again. Some undoubtedly died and were buried in the bogs; others may have found shelter in the remote glens beyond Dungloe.

When the survivors arrived in Glenties they went to the poorhouse and asked for admission. The poorhouse did not have the capacity to house all of them, and most spent the night in the rain outside. There were those who died quietly outside the poorhouse—those who were too sick, too old and too heartbroken to go on living.

The following morning a number of the Arranmore families decided to remain in the poorhouse, because they were unwilling to face the terrors of the Atlantic voyage and they preferred the humiliation of living in the poorhouse to leaving their homeland.

Those with more endurance trekked on over the mountains to Donegal Town the following day, but when they got there, they discovered the Chorley ship had yet to arrive, and the destitute islanders lay on the pier for days before the boat eventually came for them. In the meantime, the islanders would have died of hunger and exposure were it not for the food and clothing given by local residents.

No death certificates were issued for those who died on the death march from Arranmore, and it is unknown how many died on the voyage across to the United States. It is unknown either how many succumbed to grief, disease and loneliness after they arrived in the United States. But judging from the poor physical condition of those who departed, and judging from the known death rate among emigrants in similar coffin ships, as many as 20% of the people who left Donegal Town on March 6, 1848 died at sea.

Walter Chorley was responsible for all those deaths, because had he not decided to buy Arranmore and evict many of the tenants, those who died might have survived the famine.

* * *

The rent roll in Arranmore had been 200 pounds per year when Chorley took over; two years later he was taking in 900 pounds per year from only two-thirds of the holdings.

Chorley also insisted on 20% of the earnings of those who worked in the kelp industry, and he opened a store and insisted that all of his tenants shop in it.

Then he established a police barracks in Arranmore and used the police to protect him. He also had himself appointed magistrate and in this capacity he could send to jail those who defied him.

The Chorley administration of Arranmore was a dictatorship, with Chorley as resident dictator who ruled from a mansion he had built from the profits from his rents.

A plot was hatched to kill Chorley, but the Arranmore curate found out about it and persuaded the conspirators not to carry out the assassination.

But Chorley was hated so much that some looked back with nostalgia on the reign of the Marquis of Conyngham.

* * *

CHAPTER THIRTEEN

1847 has become known in popular ballads as "Black 47," as if that year of all the famine years saw the greatest distress.

But hunger and disease were also rampant in 1848 and 1849, and in some areas the worst time of all was the winter of 1848 and the spring of 1849.

Fever was rampant all over Templecrone in 1848, and in some areas, like Ranafast and Arranmore, it was causing many fatalities.[1]

Reports by Dr. Frazer Brady indicate that Templecrone was as hard hit by disease in 1848 as it was in 1847, although he indicates that he thought flu was the reasons for the widespread illness not typhus.

Still, it made very little difference to the victims whether the deaths were from flu or typhus, as the result was the same.

As the deaths continued, the inhabitants of Templecrone became increasingly indifferent to death, either their own or that of anyone else.

In late 1846, people quarreled with each other over food, but as the dying continued people became apathetic and seemed to care little whether they lived or died.

One of the by-products of this apathy was the disappearance of the Irish wake and the elaborate Irish funeral.

Prior to the famine, a wake had been a major social event that was hosted by the family of the deceased no matter how poor they were. Hundreds who came to these wakes were plied with liquor, food and tobacco, and the quality and quantity of these items was a reflection on the family. Many older people had a small hoard of money to pay for a "decent" wake and funeral.[2]

Funerals were also public events. Even the poorest person was buried in a wooden coffin and the coffin was carried through the townland on the way to the church, and the quality of the coffin had to be good, because its defects would be there for all the world to see.

Wakes and funerals were three-day events, full of rituals and important social interaction. They often defined a family's standing in the community, because the more important the family, the more lavish the wake and funeral.

The famine changed all that. Few could afford food or liquor for wakes during the famine, but even if these commodities were available, people just did not attend wakes, because of the widespread belief that one could catch the fever from a corpse.

There were few funerals either, and if there was one, only the immediate family attended.

Out in the hills and bogs beyond Dungloe, those who died were often buried in the bog without ceremony, or were buried at the bottom of the garden with other family members who had died, with no wake and no funeral.

Death had become so common that by 1848 it seemed to make no sense to fuss about it, and the disposal of bodies was prompt and without fanfare and then life went on for the survivors.

Seamus O'Donnell, of Ranafast, who was 87 in 1945, told folklore collector Hugh O'Doherty that his grandfather had seven children, five of whom died in the famine.

O'Donnell said his grandfather was very proud that he had made coffins for all five by breaking up an old boat, and that unlike the dead of other families in the area, his children were given a decent burial.

Such concern with ritual did not return to Templecrone until the 1850s.

Throughout 1848, soup kitchens were in operation in Templecrone, and they were heavily patronized.

The Relief Committee in Dungloe set up a big cauldron in the street in front of Sweeney's Hotel and made huge batches of soup from peas, turnips, potatoes, lentils, Indian corn and the bones of sheep, cows or pigs. Sometimes a calf's head or a cow's head was tossed into the cauldron with the vegetables.

During 1848, dogs and cats turned wild in the parish and would not approach humans even their former owners. A survival instinct was coming into play here, an instinct that let these animals know they ran a risk of being eaten by hungry humans.

The perception that dogs, cats and even rats were being consumed for food was widespread in the parish, and there was some basis for the perception. Many dogs and cats disappeared in late 1846 and 1847, and many people believed they had been eaten.

Nobody admitted eating one of these animals, but one man in Gweedore was seen cooking a dog and for the rest of his life was known as Manus na Mada—Manus the Dog.

The Annagry area was very hard hit in the spring of 1848, because testimonials taken from a member of the Green family of Ranafast in 1945 revealed that one small townland in the area was depopulated because of fever fatalities.

By the summer of 1848, the Poor Law Commissioners and the Relief Guardians in Glenties were suffering from battle fatigue and were becoming abrupt with those who came to them asking for relief.

At this point, there were 600 residents of the poorhouse and 12,500 on relief in the Glenties Union, which included Templecrone. Over 6,000 of those on outdoor relief were from Templecrone, almost 60% of the population and more than half of those residing in the poorhouse were also from Templecrone.[3]

Dr. Brady, who had been sympathetic with the destitute of Templecrone in 1845, 1846 and 1847, now was expressing impatience with their eternal demands, and suggested that some of them were only pretending to be sick.

Captain O'Neill, the Poor Law Commissioner, sent Conyngham's bailiffs around to check on those who were receiving relief at home to see how ill they were, and O'Neill also hired informers to keep an eye on the sick and dying in order to keep him briefed on those who died so he could cut a ration from the household.

As spring turned to summer in 1848, both those receiving aid and those giving it became confrontational. The Guardians, in Glenties, viewed those who approached them with outstretched hands with suspicion and sometimes contempt; the destitute became convinced that some of the food donated by the Quakers and the British Association was being diverted for personal use by the Guardians.

In the summer of 1848, Francis Forster asked the Poor Law Commissioners for a loan of 500 pounds which he said he would use to buy kelp from the residents of Templecrone.

Forster said that in 1847 he had kept thousands alive by employing them in the kelp business and he hoped to do the same in 1848.

But the Poor Law Commissioners refused the loan and in a written reply coldly dismissed the initiative.[4]

The Commissioners may have rejected Forster because of his relationship with Chorley, but another reason may have been that Forster borrowed 200 pounds from the Quakers in 1847 and repaid only 100 pounds.

* * *

Every nook and cranny on all the tenants' farms was set with potatoes, turnips, oats, and other vegetables in 1848, with seeds supplied by the Quakers. The whole parish prayed for a bountiful harvest.

A good harvest was a matter of life and death for Templecrone, because the British Association announced it was ending its relief efforts because of a lack of funds. The British Association had been providing half the population of Templecrone with one meal a day and without their help there would have been thousands of additional casualties in 1847 and 1848.

In June of 1848, just as the British Association was pulling out, the potato blight appeared all over Ireland again, and by July swaths of death had destroyed 90% of the potato crop but miraculously, the potato crop all over Northwest Donegal was thriving and was yielding bumper crops.

The devout Catholics of the parish, who had been praying in the fields since the blight reappeared, were sure it was a miracle that they were spared and they thanked God for protecting them.

* * *

When Prime Minister Russell heard of the latest potato failure in Ireland he was furious at the Irish for continuing to rely on the potato as a food source, as if they had a choice in the matter. He said he would do as little as possible to help them.

However, Russell was angry at the Irish for more than their dependence on potatoes. A group of Irish activists known as the Young Irelanders attempted to drive the British out of Ireland by force of arms in July of 1848, and even though the rebellion was little more than a riot, and the rebels, led by William Smith O'Brien were rounded up and jailed, the attempt at winning freedom infuriated Russell and other members of the British government, who viewed the escapade as high treason.

After that, Russell was in no mood to feed the starving Irish.

"The course of English benevolence is frozen by insult, calumny and rebellion," Russell wrote in a letter to Clarendon, the Lord Lieutenant.

The *Times* echoed Russell's sentiments, and indeed the sentiments of most of the English, on August 20th, in an editorial.

"In no country in the world have men talked treason until they are hoarse, and then gone about begging for sympathy from those they view as oppressors. In no other country have the people been so liberally helped by the nation they denounced and defied."

Neither the *Times* nor Lord John Russell would entertain the notion that it might be Britain's mismanagement of the famine crisis that was the cause of the rebellion, not the malicious character of the Irish people.

Clarendon continued to ask for assistance as the situation in Ireland became more desperate, and Russell continued to refuse to authorize public works projects or free food for the masses.

Trevelyn shut down relief headquarters in Dublin, and Routh, who had such extensive correspondence with Templecrone, left Ireland for good.

The only aid the destitute Irish could expect was Treasury loans against uncollected taxes loans that had to be paid back. Except for the aid pouring in from America, the Irish were on their own.

The British government made several other announcements in September of 1848, which would seem to have been deliberately made to inspire panic in Ireland.

The government had been asked to pick up the relief programs of the British Association which had been feeding hundreds of thousands of destitute children in the west, but Russell said no—that his government would not get involved in this activity.

Russell was then asked if he would approve the financing of another organization if that organization would agree to get food to hungry children. He said no to this too, and stated government policy against getting involved in what he believed to be the territory of the private sector.

This was the last straw for millions of Irish survivors, because they now faced the reality that the government was prepared to watch them die without lifting a finger to help them. Those who had assets of any kind turned them into cash and headed for the ports to emigrate to Canada or the United States. The great exodus from stricken Ireland had begun in earnest.

In the autumn of 1848, an act was introduced in Parliament to make it easy for landlords with large debts to sell their estates eliminating much of the red tape that had made the sales in the past a bureaucratic nightmare.

Russell hoped that debt-ridden Irish landlords would sell their property to wealthy British investors, who would in turn reorganize Irish estates the way Walter Chorley had reorganized Arranmore shipping excess people off to America and organizing the remainder into rigidly-run communities that would not be a burden to the British government.

But the new Encumbered Estates Act bore no fruit; most estates were in shambles; landlords were being murdered; and investors in England and Scotland would not buy an Irish estate at any price, because the situation in the country terrified them.

Irish revolutionary John Mitchel viewed the Encumbered Estates Act as another English plot to destroy Ireland. Mitchel believed that the Act was enacted to take title of Irish land away from the Anglo-Irish landlords and give it to English bankers. He believed that the Irish would eventually be evicted from the land and loyal British subjects would be brought in to take their place. The only thing that prevented this from taking place was the failed rebellion of 1848, which alarmed investors and discouraged new settlers.[6]

As a result, the estates were put up for sale, but there were no buyers in England or Scotland.

* * *

As the destitution increased, landlords evicted their tenants all over the country and by the end of the year more than a million homeless people tramped the roads of Ireland looking for alms.

Donegal, which escaped the potato blight in 1848, was overrun by swarms of destitute families from Connaught, who roamed the roads looking for help.

Templecrone, which had an abundant harvest of potatoes and oats, was host to ragged bands from Sligo, Galway and Mayo, who could be seen everywhere.

Help was given to these strangers, but many of them died from hunger and exposure and were buried where they fell, among the rocks and bogs.

The Templecrone tenants felt ill-equipped to provide relief for these refugees, since they were only one potato crop away from destitution themselves. But they were true to their Gaelic heritage and they shared what they had while the Connaught people remained in their midst.

In the autumn of 1848, Conyngham's bailiffs were everywhere, gathering up all the rents they could, and were demanding back rent as well.

Forster was out collecting rents, too, and like Conyngham he got most of them, although there were rents that could not be collected because of the extreme destitution of the household.

Neither landlord evicted anyone from his holding because of nonpayment of rent, however.

Chorley's tenants also paid their rent, but they had little left when they paid him, and they were not much better off than the refugees from Connaught.

My greatgrandparents, the Gallaghers of Ballintra, and my great, greatgrandparents, the Greens, also of Ballintra, lived above Walter Chorley high in the mountains. They had paid Conyngham his rents and they also gave Chorley what he demanded, but they detested him.

My grandfather, Tim Gallagher, said that his parents used to pray that Chorley's boat would capsize on the way in from Burtonport and that he would drown, and when it didn't happen his parents were convinced that the devil took care of his own.

Chorley's two oldest children died when very young and are buried in the Church of Ireland graveyard in Maghery. Their death must have brought home to him the grief suffered by those who lost children in the famine or because of the evictions of the Arranmore tenants.

CHAPTER FOURTEEN

In many ways, 1849 was Black '47 revisited. Hunger and fever swept over much of Ireland and fresh rounds of evictions took place all over the country. Ireland continued to be abandoned by its people as the ports were choked with families trying to get out of the country.

Dublin and other major cities were being compared to 19th century African cities, full of beggars and invalids. The Irish economy was nonexistent and there were those who believed it would never recover.

Even the *Times*, which had been an opponent of aid to Ireland changed its views. On February 8, 1849, it advocated relief for the most distressed areas, especially those areas where armies of beggars roamed the countryside with nothing to eat.

Instead of giving aid directly to the most distressed areas, Russell came up with another new way of financing Irish relief. This time he proposed that those areas that had not suffered extreme distress be levied with additional taxes to pay for famine relief in destitute areas. Loans would be advanced to send food to feed the destitute areas, but the bill would be paid by any area that might be able to pay it.

The reaction to the new scheme was negative all over Ireland, and it even made allies out of Nationalists and Orangemen, who believed they had better unite to oppose the plan, before the middle class became as destitute as the beggars who roamed the roads.

Chief Poor Law Commissioner Twisleton, who had served Russell loyally throughout the famine, resigned because he said the government had a policy of genocide towards the Irish and as a man of honor he did not want to be part of it.[1]

But in spite of all the opposition, the new law, entitled Rate in Aid Act, was passed by the British Parliament, and the troops and the tax collectors were out in force once again.

Templecrone was given additional aid because of this new law to help feed the beggars from outside the area who had come into Templecrone again in droves, and relief was also given to residents who had not yet recovered from the hunger of previous years.

By this time, however, the people of Templecrone were recovering their strength, and there was little hunger among the majority of them in the summer of 1849. Indeed, the people of the area were better off than some resident landlords in other parts of Ireland who were living in dilapidated mansions and eating rabbits and boiled nettles in order to survive.

It took very little to raise the standard of living of Templecrone farmers back up to what it was prior to the famine, since all they had then was an abundance of potatoes, and given an abundance of potatoes again they were as well off as they had ever been.

But the people had learned some bitter lessons since 1845 and a change had come over them because of the horrors they had experienced.

Many of the tenants were now saving all they could, even if it involved cutting down on the amount of potatoes consumed, and they were selling the potatoes and other food they had accumulated for cash, and the reason for this was that they were determined to earn enough money to pay their fares to America.

The thought of emigration was entirely new in this part of Donegal, because for centuries the inhabitants of Templecrone had clung doggedly to their rock-strewn patches of land and neither war nor persecution had driven them out of those hills.

But the horrors of 1846, 1847, and 1848 had alienated many of them from the life they were leading and made them determined to abandon this place and find a new life in another country.

Most had not accumulated the price of fares for entire families until the early 1850s, when the first emigrants left, but within a few years there was a steady stream of people leaving. This exodus continued long after the famine was a dim memory.

Templecrone was fortunate to have an abundant food supply in 1849, because on June 5th, the Quakers announced that they would no longer be involved in the relief of the destitute in Ireland.

The Quaker announcement came as a surprise, because Ireland as a whole was in desperate straits, and in many areas this religious group was the only source of assistance that countless thousands could rely on. Their dedication, energy and compassion had brought relief to millions of Irish famine victims.

But the Quakers had for some time been overwhelmed by the sheer magnitude of the destitution in Ireland, and increasingly alienated from the Russell government whom they believed was doing very little to support their relief efforts, and was instead involved in what seemed like a policy of extermination.

The last straw for the Quakers was a letter from Charles Trevelyn to the organization on June 2, 1849. The following is the letter which precipitated the Quaker departure.

"Lord John Russell has desired me to enquire from you what plan the Relief Committee of the Society of Friends is now pursuing for the relief of the serious distress which still prevails in some of the western districts of Ireland; and to express to you his willingness to contribute one hundred pounds towards the object. I do this with much satisfaction, as besides the good that would be done [with this gift] it affords a proof of his lordship's continued and, I must add, well deserved confidence in your society.

Signed C.E. Trevelyn"

One can imagine the reaction of the Quaker leaders in Dublin, who saw the country in ruins and millions on the edge of eternity, to a letter from the only person in the United Kingdom who had the power to provide massive and immediate help, but who was instead offering a personal donation of 100 pounds and inquiring of the Quakers what they were going to do about the horrors that were abroad. It was the last straw.

Quaker leader Jonathan Pim's reply to Trevelyn was a model of control, but in it he stated some basic truths and let the British leadership know what he thought about a number of issues.[2]

It was Pim's opinion that a calamity such as this was not something that could be handled by private resources that it was well beyond the ability of any organization to cope with.

"The government alone could raise funds or carry out the measures in many districts to save the lives of the people."

Pim went on to state that his organization did not want to begin a task that was beyond its capabilities.

"We fear that if we venture to undertake a work for which our resources are so inadequate, we might, through our incompetence, injure the causes of those we desire to serve."

Pim's strategy was to put the responsibility on Russell for dealing with the situation, and he no doubt believed that if the Quakers backed out that the British government would be forced to fill the vacuum created by the departure of the Quakers.

He was wrong. Russell ignored Pim's letter and refused to offer any help.

* * *

The British were being criticized all over the world for the way they were responding to the Irish tragedy, but the British were so powerful on the world stage at this time that they did not care what any other nation thought of them.

However, when Clarendon told Russell that it would be a good idea to have a major distraction on the Irish scene, such as a visit from Queen Victoria, Russell thought this a good idea, as it would provide valuable public relations for England.

So, the Queen came to Ireland in the summer of 1849 as part of a carefully managed propaganda exercise to dupe the world into believing that the Irish were happy under British rule and they just loved the "Queen of Ireland."[3]

Queen Victoria visited Cork, Dublin and Kildare during her stay, and saw neither the dying nor the dead, but only happy welcoming faces.

Many of Ireland's Anglo-Irish aristocrats boycotted the receptions, because they were furious at Russell's ploy, and some suggested she be taken out into the countryside to see the armies of beggars and the dead bodies piled outside the poorhouses.

Other Anglo-Irish aristocrats accused Russell of being cynical and corrupt for staging exotic banquets while Ireland starved.

Out in the Irish countryside nothing changed because of the Royal visit and the dying continued.

In distant Templecrone, there was no excitement about the Queen's visit to Dublin. Dublin was so far away that very few had ever been there and the vast majority had no idea what a big city looked like, never mind the excitement created by a Royal visit.

* * *

Most histories of the famine give 1849 as the year the famine ended. Whether or not this is accurate depends on which definition of "the famine" one uses.

If the famine is defined as the failure of the potato crop, then 1849, with its abundance of potatoes in late summer, can be called the year when the famine ended.

But in late summer 1849, even while the potatoes bloomed in the fields and baskets of healthy potatoes were being brought out of the ground, there were more than a million displaced persons in Ireland who had set no crop and who had, therefore, no potatoes to dig. The famine was far from over for them.

A much more comprehensive description than the potato famine is needed to describe this period in Ireland a description which encompasses the potato blight, the fever, the evictions, the emigration and the economic ruin which began in 1845 and continued for many years after the years of the blight.

The National Library in Dublin has recognized that "potato famine" is not an appropriate description for events in Ireland during this period, and has filed much of the material under the label distress. Distress was the word the English used to describe the situation in Ireland, and during the first half of the 19th century there were numerous parliamentary studies of "distressed districts in Ireland" and collections of documents on the subject were entitled "Distress Papers."

Distress is a vague word that is too broad to describe the period, but it is certainly better than potato famine, which does not accurately describe the period at all.

There is a great deal of confusion today about when the famine began and when it ended. Black '47 is often mentioned, as if this was the year when the Irish really suffered; then, the years 1847, 1848 and 1849 are often given as the three years when the destitution was greatest.

But in Templecrone, the suffering began in 1845, when one third of the families lost all their food supply when the potato blight struck, and 1846 was a year of great hunger, disease and brutal weather conditions, and many lives were lost in this period. 1847 was, of course, disastrous in Templecrone and so was the first half of 1848. And even though there were potatoes in the parish from this period onwards, people were still dying from fever and completely traumatized for years afterwards by the loss of children, parents and other family members.

So, the famine in Templecrone, was not a one or two year event, and it involved a great deal more than just a failure of the potato crop.

* * *

CHAPTER FIFTEEN

The *Times* sent a reporter back to Templecrone in 1850 to investigate how the parish was doing in the aftermath of the famine years. He published a lengthy story on the parish in January.[1]

The reporter found an abundance of potatoes, oats and barley and no shortage of food of any kind. He even wrote that barley was being used to make homemade whiskey, an activity that had ceased in the area since 1845.

In Dungloe, on market day, there was a wide variety of handmade items of clothing for sale, and buyers from Derry and Sligo were on hand to purchase them for the London market.

The reporter discovered that rent was being paid in the parish once again and that the people looked healthy.

But behind that facade of recovery and outward appearance of good health were wounds in the psyche which would never heal, and which would, during the next 20 years cause thousands of these people to close their homes in Templecrone and book a fare to America, turning their backs on their homeland forever.

The failure of the potato crop had set in motion a sequence of events that had included death and immeasurable grief, but the people might have recovered from these wounds were it not for their conviction that it could happen again and they would still have no way to defend themselves from such devastation.

Back in 1846, the people had believed that the government would eventually come to their rescue once it realized the enormity of the tragedy that was taking place.

But they had learned since then that the government would never help them and would let them die, and so many were determined to live their lives out in a different land where a government offered protection, not persecution.

It was the younger people with small children who first made the decision to abandon Templecrone. These young people did not want to see their children die in the same agonizing way that youngsters had died from fever and starvation in 1846, 1847 and 1848.

The young parents were terrified of the long arduous voyage to America, but the fear of famine was even greater and a decision was made to cross the Atlantic.

The thriftiness that was first seen in 1849 continued in 1850 and for a number of years afterwards, as families gathered the funds necessary to buy the fares, and for the reserve of money needed to tide them over until they got jobs once they arrived in America.

Some families impatient to be on their way, sent the father or older sons out to the United States first to earn money which was then sent home to bring other members of the family out.

In the Campbell family, two great grand uncles, John and Alec Campbell, emigrated to the coal mining regions of Pennsylvania in 1854 and established homes in Tamaqua and Tuscarora.

When they were well established in the 1860s, they brought out three nephews and two nieces: Alec, James, Thomas, Sarah and Annie Campbell, all of whom settled in the same area.

The younger Alec Campbell was to become a prominent personality in the Molly Maguire saga in Carbon County, in the 1870s, and was executed on June 21, 1877, in Mauch Chunk.

Scores of other family members Sweeneys, Boyles, Gallaghers, Wards and Dohertys also fled Templecrone in the 1850s and 1860s and settled in New York, New Jersey, Pennsylvania and Massachusetts, and only a few ever returned home again.

They left Ireland traumatized by the horrors they had endured and were unforgiving in their animosity towards the British rulers of Ireland.

In driving the Irish people out of Ireland, the British leaders did not succeed in eliminating Irish animosity to England they merely dispersed the hate across the Atlantic, and the animosity of the Irish in America has haunted the British ever since.

In the decades that followed the famine, Templecrone became an incubator for the Irish colonies in America. Parents still raised big families, but even if a couple had 10 children, they would be very lucky if one of them remained at home.

In the decades after the famine, emigration did to Templecrone what hunger, disease and murderous landlords had never been able to do—it reduced the population dramatically.

By 1875, Templecrone had only half the population it had in 1846, and by the end of the century the population had dropped to 25% of what it had been on the eve of the famine.

County Donegal, as a whole, dropped from approximately 300,000 in 1846 to less than 100,000 by the turn of the century. All of this decline was directly related to the famine.

The population of Templecrone is now slowly beginning to increase again, but the immigration syndrome is still evident and the youth of Templecrone still head out of the parish once they are old enough to work.

Nobody grows potatoes or barley or oats anymore—all these commodities are bought in the stores, and some are imported from abroad.

The area enjoyed a brief era of prosperity in the 80s, 90s, and in the early years of this century, with the establishment of factories in the area and the growth of the fishing industry, but then came the economic crash which closed factories, hotels, and sent the young people of the area off to Australia, New Zealand and Canada looking for work, just as their ancestors did in the 19th century.

* * *

The cost of the famine to the people of Templecrone cannot just be measured by the number of people who died or emigrated, or the grief endured by those who survived. The whole fabric of Gaelic society was impacted and it never reverted to what it was prior to the famine.

In the 1840s, the vast majority of the inhabitants of the area, including the resident landlord, Conyngham's agent, and the clergymen of all denominations spoke Irish they had to in order to communicate with the inhabitants, most of whom had very little English.

But in the aftermath of the famine, when many families were planning to get out of Templecrone and emigrate to either Canada or the United States, a knowledge of English was considered crucial, because those who spoke only Irish would be unable to communicate at all abroad and would be unable to find employment or become easily integrated into their new homeland.

Therefore, many adults learned English and they then taught English to their children, and the result of this was that a majority of the people acquired knowledge of English, even though most of them still used Irish when communicating with each other.

In the decades after the famine English replaced Irish as the primary language in Maghery, Dungloe, Burtonport and other areas along the coast, but Irish survived in the interior of the parish, in the hills, and in the Ranafast area. It still survives there today.

Tim Gallagher, my grandfather, was born in Arranmore in the 1850s and spoke mostly Irish growing up there. But he married a girl named Brigid Doherty from Meenmore, near Dungloe, who was born in the 1860s and spoke little Irish, and when the couple married and set up a home on Innisfree

Island, they spoke only English to each other and raised seven children, none of whom spoke Irish.

I once asked him why he did not speak Irish anymore and he was surprised by the question.

"Who would I speak it to," he said. "Your grandmother does not speak it and nobody in Innisfree speaks it. Would you want me to talk to myself in Irish?"

The cultural tragedy that was personified in my grandfather was that he saw no point in expressing himself in the old language because it no longer served any useful purpose.

He would later boast that all of his seven children went off to the United States fluent in the English language and that this gave them a competitive edge over the immigrants from Russia, Italy and Germany.

English made inroads into the Irish-speaking community for another reason. All through the famine the Anglo-Irish and English newspapers referred to Irish as the language of a backward people, and subconsciously many Irish speakers believed that when they learned English they were taking a step upwards on the social ladder.

The third reason for the triumph of English over Irish in the aftermath of the famine was the establishment of primary schools in Templecrone, which encouraged the use of English among children, and penalized those who could not communicate in this language.

Irish, therefore, was under attack on a number of fronts after the famine, and while it still survives in Templecrone, the language of the majority is now English.

* * *

The famine had a negative impact on the Gaelic custom of offering hospitality to any stranger who knocked on a door. Wanderers who had been warmly greeted before the famine were given an icy welcome afterwards and often given no alms at all.

The tramps and tinkers had once been a valuable source of news about the outside world and a reservoir of songs and folk tales which they had recited to entertain their hosts. But after the famine, the people in Templecrone were in no mood for entertainment, because the horrors they had endured left them with no appreciation of songs or poetry and it took decades before music and song became part of their lives again.

In many areas friendships between neighbors and even relatives were destroyed because of feuds that erupted during the famine. These feuds sometimes went on for generations.

In 1945, for instance, Johnny Jimmie Frank (O'Donnell) of Burtonport, spoke bitterly to a folklore collector about Johndy Sweeney, who owned Sweeney's Hotel Dungloe during the famine. O'Donnell accused Sweeney of seizing small holdings from farmers who had been extended credit during the famine and not repaid their debt.

Yet an examination of the records for 1857 indicates that Sweeney had only modest holdings and did not appear to have acquired the holdings of any other tenant farmer.

The reality of Johndy Sweeney's activities during the famine was that he had invested his life's savings in the hotel prior to the famine and then saw it all put at risk because of the credit he had extended in 1845 and 1846. He returned to the Missouri River after the famine and it was the money he made during this period that enabled his business to survive, not black market prices or property seized from destitute tenants.[3]

Yet, like all small businessmen he was accused after the famine of questionable business practices, and the accusation was alive and well a hundred years later.

* * *

Ill will continued for generations among neighbors who nursed grievances over issues that emerged during the famine.

Some families held grudges against other families over the failure of one family to come to the aid of another family, who had been friends and neighbors prior to the famine.

Feuds erupted over sheep stealing or the theft of turnips, and often there was no proof of who committed the crime, and accusations were made without proof.

People from the hills above Dungloe nursed a bitterness against those who lived along the seashore over disputes that arose when the coast dwellers resented that "their" cockles and mussels were being picked by the people from the hills during the worst of the destitution. Shellfish had never been on the diet of those who lived in the interior until the famine years, and those who lived on the coast resented an invasion of outsiders.

The bailiffs and subagents of Conyngham were generally shunned because of the seizure of livestock and grain during the famine, and their descendants had to bear the burden of their heritage for generations.

A hundred years after the famine, storytellers still talked with contempt about a subagent named Boyle, who was more vicious than Robert Russell, and they talked about his sons who became subagents to Forster and who were as mean as their father. There had always been friction between individuals and families in Templecrone prior to the famine, but the dissension that erupted after the famine far exceeded normal friction and was caused by the unusual stress put on the community by the years of hunger and death.

* * *

CHAPTER SIXTEEN

When historians examine the question of who was responsible for the devastation caused by the famine, the answers given depend on the viewpoint of the historian.

A small minority of historians, who have fundamentalist Christian beliefs, accept the view expressed by Sir Charles Trevelyn that the famine was a disaster visited on the Irish by God and that the British government did all it could to bring relief to the Irish given the magnitude of the disaster.

Then, there are a few who echo Lord John Russell's sentiments that the Irish had only themselves to blame for becoming so dependent on the potato that its failure caused a catastrophe.

The failure of the Irish to survive on the fish that swarmed along the coast has been an issue for many historians the implication being that they starved while in the presence of an abundance of food.

There are also those who argue that the landlords were to blame for the disaster, and that all of the deaths should be placed at their doorstep.

A popular argument among Irish nationalists is that the disaster was engineered by the British government, who used the potato failure to break the back of Irish nationalism and vastly reduce the population.

And there are combinations of these viewpoints, ranging from a complete exoneration of the British to an indictment of Lord John Russell as the Adolph Hitler of the 19th century.

* * *

What, if any, is the validity of any of these viewpoints as far as the famine experience in Templecrone is concerned? An analysis of these viewpoints one by one provides some answers.

Trevelyn's view that the famine was an act of God cannot be debated, since only God knows the answer to that question. But his statement that the government did all it could to help Templecrone is just not true, because without private aid the inhabitants would have perished, and government aid was minimal and was in the form of a loan. Trevelyn and Routh had in fact consistently refused to come to the aid of Templecrone, even when informed by Griffith, Forster, McMenamin and the Quakers that hundreds had died and thousands were at risk, and their response had always been a refusal to help no matter what the consequences.

So, the position taken by Trevelyn that all was done that could be done was inaccurate as far as the situation in Templecrone was concerned.

Russell's position that the Irish had only themselves to blame for their dependence on the potato was only a valid position if the Irish tenant farmers had other options which they did not exercise.

The reality was that the people of Templecrone relied on the potato because this was the only food that could yield all the nutrients needed to sustain life and also yielded far more food per acre than any other food.

Given large Irish families and the intense competition for land, most subtenants had no choice in the matter: the potato was the only crop that could sustain life for those who only had an acre or a half acre at their disposal. Had they grown oats on their potato patches, they would have starved to death even in the best of times. The irony of Russell's statements, which were made in the summer of 1848, was that some of the Templecrone tenants, like my Green and Gallagher ancestors in Arranmore and my Campbell ancestors in Dungloe, each of which had more than 10 acres rented, planted fields of turnips in 1848 as an insurance against the failure of the potato crop and then watched as their turnip crop was wiped out by a blight, while the potato crop flourished. Had they switched from potatoes to turnips they would have starved.

The question of how people in coastal areas like Donegal could die of hunger while the sea around them teamed with fish can only be understood by those who are familiar with the fishing industry in Donegal at that time.

The coast along Templecrone faces a very turbulent Atlantic Ocean, and the coast itself is strewn with rugged islands and rocks just below the waterline. This makes navigation in the area extremely dangerous.

The vast majority of the boats used by those who lived along the shoreline at that time were flimsy curraghs, which were good for fishing within the shelter of bays and inlets, but totally impractical for fishing in the open sea where the great shoals of fish were.

The Templecrone fishermen could not afford to build big sturdy boats capable of deep sea fishing, nor could they afford the expensive nets and tackle needed for these boats, because after they had paid the landlord his rent, they had very few resources left to invest in anything.

So, fishing for the men of Burtonport and Arranmore was an activity that brought additional food to the table, and when the shoals of fish occasionally moved into the bays and inlets, it even put some money in their pockets. But during the famine the shoals of fish stayed well out at sea, and the fishermen, who could not feed their families on the limited number of fish caught in the bays, sold their boats and gear to buy food for their families.

After the famine, in 1850, the *Times* reported that great shoals of sprat had moved into the bays and inlets in the Inver area of South Donegal, and fishermen were taking them out of the water in extraordinary quantities. Sprat was being offered at three pence for a hundred pounds and these fish were so cheap and plentiful that tenant farmers were spreading them all over their fields as fertilizer.

Had such an incredible abundance of fish been available in Templecrone during 1846 and 1847 there would have been no deaths from hunger. Or if the people had the fishing equipment to go 20 or 30 miles out to sea they would not have starved either. As it was, they died because of circumstances beyond their control.

* * *

Traditionally, Irish landlords have been characterized as the bogeymen of the Irish famine: they were believed to be merciless tyrants who extracted the last penny from their tenants and, on occasion, evicted sick tenants in the middle of winter and caused their deaths.

This is an accurate characterization of some Irish landlords, but it is not an accurate portrait of all of them, and the landlord experience in Templecrone is an indication of how complex this issue really is.

The four landlords who controlled Templecrone between 1845 and 1850 were the Marquis of Conyngham, Francis Forster, Walter Chorley and the Reverend Valentine Griffith.

While the experience of the tenants under each of these landlords during the famine does not represent the tenant-and-landlord experience all over Ireland, the difference in the way these landlords behaved illustrates the fact that very few generalities can be made about Irish landlords, and that the only way to judge them, is to judge them one at a time on the basis of their merits, or sins of omission.

If one was to define an ideal Irish landlord, then the traits displayed by the Church of Ireland minister, Reverend Valentine Pole Griffith, would serve as a benchmark to judge other landlords.

Griffith did not evict any of his tenants; he worked tirelessly to raise money to feed the destitute in his parish; he and his wife nursed the dying, giving them comfort; and helped bury the dead, most of whom were not of his faith. He was in fact a preacher who practiced what he preached.

Francis Forster, who had 400 tenants, was a man of contradictions.

Before the famine, Forster and his father before him had been loyal agents of the Marquis of Conyngham, and after that he had been a ruthless and effective agent for Lord George Hill, helping him evict hundreds of tenants. Prior to the famine he had built up a considerable estate for himself and had no hesitation in raising rents or evicting tenants.

In 1850, a group of his tenants in Annagry petitioned the Lord Lieutenant to protect them from the way he was raising their rents and seizing their livestock when they refused to pay, but the Lord Lieutenant took Forster's side and sent police to Annagry to help him subdue his rebellious tenants.

However, during the famine, from October of 1845 to the spring of 1848, Forster was a model landlord who raised a great deal of money to feed the hungry, and there is no doubt that without his efforts Templecrone would have been turned into a vast graveyard.

Into the final judgment on Forster must go his probably involvement with the Arranmore evictions. There is little evidence that he conspired with Chorley in this affair, but it is unlikely that Chorley would have purchased Arranmore without Forster's approval, and so Forster must bear some blame for what happened after the evictions.

It is ironic that Forster, who worked so hard for three years to keep the people of Arranmore alive, should have conspired to betray them in the end with fatal consequences.

The betrayal of the Arranmore tenants does not cancel the credit earned by Forster for the thousands of lives he saved, but this betrayal underlines the complex nature of the man and the difficulty of making generalizations about him.

* * *

There is little complexity about the aristocratic Conyngham he simply took care of his own interests and cared nothing about what happened to his tenants.

But was Conyngham responsible for the devastation in Templecrone? Did he cause it? Could he have prevented it? And what degree of blame, if any, must be assigned to him.

Obviously, Conyngham was not responsible for the potato blight, and the only issues that impact on the distress that occurred were Conyngham's management of his estate and his failure to contribute to the relief effort.

There is no question that Conyngham managed his estates very badly and this mismanagement set the stage for his tenants to depend heavily on the potato as a sole source of food.

However, in fairness, Conyngham inherited this style of management from his father and his grandfather, and it was a type of mismanagement all too common throughout Ireland. The problem was that a landlord-tenant system had been in place for centuries in Ireland, and it was this system that needed to be corrected and not the shortcomings of individual landlords.

Could Conyngham have saved the lives of hundreds if he had contributed heavily to famine relief from the very beginning? Probably. Had he been willing to sell off some of his assets or borrow heavily he could have bought the food needed to save the lives of his tenants, but the enormity of the cost over a four-year period would probably have made him bankrupt.

This in turn raises another issue. Was it really the responsibility of the landlords to bear the burden of famine relief, or was the British government responsible and not the landlords.

Conyngham claimed during the famine that he was not making any money on his Templecrone estate that all the rents went to London bankers who had advanced money to Conyngham's father, and the rents were going to pay off this debt.

Furthermore, Conyngham argued that he could not be held responsible for a major catastrophe like this, and that no landlord could cope with it, even if he were affluent.

Finally, he claimed that the British government was making him a scapegoat for its own failure to provide relief, and that Russell and his aides were responsible for the tragedy, not him.

The Quaker leaders, who had little respect for Conyngham or any landlord like him, agreed with him on this last issue. Pim, the Quaker leader, believed ultimate responsibility lay with Russell, and, that landlords were being made scapegoats to draw attention away from the sins of the British government.

* * *

The track record of the landlords in Templecrone was mixed: two of them did what they could to help, one of them did nothing, and the fourth Chorley acted like the evil landlord of Irish folklore.

In the next parish to the south, Lettermacaward, the major resident landlord, Colonel Conolly, did all he could to help his tenants and even used his own funds to buy food when no other funds were available.

In the parish to the north, Lord George Hill, like Forster, made every effort to get relief into the area, but he never used any of his own funds, and his record on the whole is mixed.

Given the variety of ways that Donegal landlords behaved during the famine the myth of the evil landlord has little basis in reality. It would seem that only a minority were like Walter Chorley, and the rest of them, even those like Conolly or Valentine Griffith, were stuck with that type of reputation, whether they deserved it or not.

* * *

Who was to blame, then, for Ireland's agony? Irish nationalists have rejected the landlord argument, and also rejected the laisse faire defense that it was the economic system that was to blame. Instead they blame Prime Minister Russell, because he had the power to prevent the tragedy, and did not, and therefore he bears full responsibility for what happened.

This is the most logical argument because it is an argument that can be supported by documentation.

And the laisse faire defense can be quickly demolished by the following question: "Would Russell still have adhered to the laisse faire doctrine if the great hunger had taken place in England?"

* * *

CHAPTER SEVENTEEN

It is not known how many people died in Ireland during the famine or how many emigrated. Official British estimates of population decline between 1841 and 1851 range from 1.6 million to 2.5 million. These numbers include both deaths and emigration. Irish estimates of population decline range from 3 million to 4.5 million.

The census of 1841 showed 8,175,124 people in Ireland, and the census of 1851 showed a population of 6,552,385 a decline of 1,622,739. These are the statistics that are the most commonly used to calculate the cost of the famine, and they are usually broken into an estimated 500,000 dead and 1.1 million emigrated.

However, there is a footnote to the 1851 census that estimates that the 1841 population should have increased to 9,018,799 by the autumn of 1846, so the decline between December of 1846 and the spring of 1851 was almost 2.5 million. This is a footnote that is often overlooked by historians.

But in calculating the increase from 1841 to 1846, the census commissioners projected only a 10% population increase between 1841 and late 1846, which seems a low estimate, since the population had been increasing at an average of 2.5% per year since 1821, and there was no reason to believe this rate of increase had not continued from 1841 to the beginning of 1847. A more accurate estimate by the British Census Commissioners would have been a population of 9.5 million at the beginning of 1847, and the decline therefore would have been almost 3 million.

However, as Cecil Woodham Smith revealed in *The Great Hunger*, this estimate is also open to question, because she discovered that many sub-tenants were not counted in the 1841 census, and because of this she believed the population was more than 10 million. This could have increased the population decline to almost 4 million.

The estimates of the number of people who emigrated range from one million to 2 million, because one set of statistics includes all those who left Irish ports, regardless of their destination, while another set includes only those who departed for North America.

No accurate estimate of how many people died or how many people emigrated is possible since it is unknown how many people were in the country in late 1846, and without an accurate estimate for that number it is not possible to estimate the number of dead, or the number who departed the country.

However, if a high estimate of 1.5 million is given for those who emigrated, then the death count could range from 1.5 million to 3 million, depending on the number of people who were actually in Ireland in January 1847.

Another problem: Irish rebel John Mitchel accused the British government of manipulating the 1851 census to cover up the extent of the carnage. He stated that there were a million fewer people in Ireland than the census indicated, and if this was true then another million would have been added to the death count.

* * *

It is as difficult to get an accurate estimate of the casualties in Templecrone as it is for the rest of Ireland.

In the census of 1841, the population of Templecrone was given as 9,852, and with a normal rate of increase it would have been 11,330 in late 1846. The population in the 1851 census is shown as 9,542, a decline of 1,787, or 15.5%.

If the 1841 census was accurate and the 1851 census had not been manipulated, then the death count could be determined by deducting those who were evicted from Arranmore by Chorley from the 1,787 number.

According to local legend, Chorley evicted "half the population" of Arranmore in March of 1848, and if this is accurate the problem then becomes to estimate the population of Arranmore at the beginning of 1848. When this number is arrived at, it can be divided in half, and that half is the number of people that Chorley evicted from Arranmore.

This same number should then be deducted from the number that represents the total decline in population in Templecrone by 1851—1,787 and the remainder would be the death count for the parish during the famine years.

This would seem to be a relatively simple procedure until the census data for 1841 and 1851 is analyzed, and one tries to reconcile this data with the death count of 500 for Arranmore estimated by Mrs. Valentine Griffith in 1849 in a letter to Anseth Nicholson. Then, major problems emerge.

The census of 1841 showed Arranmore with a population of 1,500 a number that would have increased to 1,725 by the end of 1846. The census of 1851 showed a population of 1,400, which is a decline of 325.

Obviously this is well below the 500 death count estimated by Mrs. Valentine Griffith, and it makes no allowance at all for the Chorley evictions.

Since the 500 body count seems to be compatible with the destruction in Arranmore described by the Quakers and other witnesses, and even if the deaths were only half that amount, the 325 decline based on the census data would still not include the Chorley evictions, and the conclusion one must draw is that the 1841 census data or the 1851 census data was inaccurate.

A clue to which census data was inaccurate can be found in the Thomas Campbell Foster article on Arranmore published in the *Times* of London in September of 1845. Inadvertently, Foster provided information that is at odds with the 1841 census.

In the article, Foster reveals that Arranmore was swarming with sub-tenants who had erected an additional dwelling, and sometimes two dwellings, on the holding of every tenant of record, and if one examines the census of 1841, only the tenants of record are counted, and the sub-tenants are ignored.

This is the same practice noted by Cecil Woodham Smith in *The Great Hunger*, who stated that some absentee landlords in the west of Ireland, who thought they had a tenant population of 10,000, discovered they had 40,000 when they were asked to provide relief for them during the famine.

When Thomas Campbell Foster visited Arranmore in 1845, he spent most of the day in the townland near the pier a townland named Leabgarrow.

Foster interviewed people who lived in Leabgarrow and he also provided a description of the people and their dwellings. He even counted the dwellings: 124 in all.

Campbell Foster described Leabgarrow as a graphic example of the evils of subletting. He stated that families had sublet plots of land and erected shacks on them, and around these shacks were swarms of children. He stated that the entire village was overcrowded and poverty stricken.

Foster's description is at odds with the description of Leabgarrow in the 1841 census, which listed only 48 dwellings in the townland, each with a 3 to 4 acre plot of land attached. It is at odds also with the 1851 census which listed 38 dwellings in the same townland.

The only possible explanation for the discrepancies is that when the 1841 census was taken all the subtenants and their droves of children were not counted, which means that a total of 78 dwellings were unaccounted for in Leabgarrow in the 1841 census all of them subtenants. Since both the 1841 and 1851 census indicated that the average household in Arranmore contained 5.7 persons, the 78 dwellings not counted represent 445 missing people.

T. Campbell Foster did not count the dwellings in the other townlands in Arranmore, but if it is assumed that each of the tenants in Arranmore had at least one subtenant dwelling on their plot, then it can be estimated that the population of Arranmore was at least twice the official count for 1841 namely a population of 3,000 people, which increased to 3,400 by late 1846.

If these new estimates for 1841 and 1846 are used and the official count of 1,400 is used for 1851, then the 500 death count given by Mrs. Griffith in 1849 and the eviction of half the population by Chorley would seem to make sense.

If the population was 3,400 in 1846 and 500 died in 1846, 1847 and early 1848, there would have been 2,900 left in March of 1848 when Chorley evicted all the subtenants. If Chorley evicted half the survivors 1,450 people there would have been 1,450 left, and if another 50 died in the spring and summer of 1848, then the balance left would be 1,400 which is the same as the official count for 1851.

Again, these numbers only agree with one another if the actual count for Arranmore in 1841 is twice the official count, because the death count given by Rev Griffith and the commonly accepted account of the Chorley evictions are totally at odds with the official census.

All of this has implications for the population estimates for the rest of Templecrone on the eve of the famine, and, indeed, for the estimates of how many died or emigrated from Templecrone as a result of the famine.

If there were 1,700 additional people in Arranmore on the eve of the famine than had previously been estimated, then the previous estimate of 11,330 for the population of Templecrone needs to be bumped up 1,700 to 13,030. And if there were 13,030 people in Templecrone in late 1846 and only 9,542 there in 1851, the population decline was 3,488, not 1,787. If 1,450 of this 3,488 represent the Chorley evictions, then the death count was 2,038.

But even this estimated death count could be low, because it is based on the subtenants not being counted in just Arranmore. What if there were thousands of subtenants not counted on Conyngham's estate in the rest of Templecrone? Then these numbers would have to be added to the death count and the death count could be double 2,038, or even more.

This high death toll in Templecrone seems incredible given the fact that local historians in modern times were convinced that there had been very few casualties. Yet there are discrepancies in the Census numbers for 1841 and 1851 which, when combined with the Chorley evictions, the documentation provided by the Mrs. Griffith of Maghery, and the expose of the *Times* journalist Campbell Foster, which clearly indicates that there was a high death toll,

How could this catastrophe have occurred and yet have none of it seep down into the folklore?

How could my father and my grandfather, both of whom were deeply interested in local history have no knowledge of this history?

The only way this could have happened is for there have been a widespread denial among the survivors about the extent of the tragedy and an unwillingness by the survivors to talk about it to their children and their grandchildren.

On a separate issue: one can only speculate why the subtenants were not counted. One possibility is that Conyngham's agents were taking bribes for ignoring the subtenants and since it was the agents and bailiffs who also supervised the census taking, it would be very easy for them to misrepresent the number of people on the estate in 1841.

In the final analysis, it would be a mistake to overestimate the importance of whether the death count in Templecrone was 250 or 4,000. Once those type of numbers are reached it is relatively unimportant to dwell on statistics and get bogged down in debates about the number of people who lost their lives.

The horror in the famine in Northwest Donegal is not in the numbers, but in the way they died, because as Francis Forster stated in 1847, when describing death in Templecrone, death by hunger is the most terrible of all deaths "so slow, yet so certain."

That slow agonizing death of men, women and little children is the real horror and this should be the focus of any study of the famine.

* * *

CHAPTER EIGHTEEN

The lack of folklore on the local level is not unique to Templecrone—all over Ireland there is a similar scarcity of folklore, as if the famine had been erased from the group memory, as something best forgotten about.

Some modern historians claims that the lack of folklore is an indication that the Irish are deliberately suppressing the memory of the famine that they are in fact exhibiting classic symptoms of group denial. Many Jews prefer not to talk about the Holocaust, and were it not for the work of dedicated Jewish activists, the Holocaust might not have been as widely publicized as it has.

It would take a parish-by-parish audit of Ireland to determine whether or not this theory of total denial is accurate, but as far as Templecrone is concerned, this theory is well off the mark, since my extensive investigation revealed that most of the people did not know anything about what happened in Templecrone—they were not in denial, they were just unaware of what had taken place.

There are three reasons why there was a scarcity of information in Templecrone about what happened in the parish during the famine.

The first, and probably the most important reason, is that those who survived the famine were so traumatized by what they had endured that they told their children who had been born after the famine very little about what had happened.

The reaction is understandable. Parents who lost their children and saw them buried in bog holes, or lost their parents from hunger and watched them die slowly, were so devastated by their experience that they were reluctant to talk about it afterwards, not even to their children.

Shame and guilt also keep the survivors silent.

The survivors experienced a great deal of guilt for surviving when loved ones died. They were convinced that their survival was at the expense of others, and the survivors who saw their children die were especially traumatized.

The survivors were also plagued by feelings of shame that the famine had reduced them to the level of beggars who were dependent on others for every morsel of bread.

The memories of lining up at the soup kitchens humiliated many of them, and for those who were forced to find refuge in the poorhouse in Glenties, the feelings of shame lasted a lifetime.

All of these emotions were suppressed and were buried deep in the psyche, and as a defense mechanism against these emotions, the survivors rarely talked about the horrors they had been through, and in order to protect their newborn children from the burden of such emotions, they either said nothing about the famine, or, as was the case in Templecrone, they denied what had happened and told their children that there was little distress in the area.

The fact that the newspapers circulating in Templecrone during the famine represented the interests of the landlords and the British government provides a second reason why so little information was handed down from this period. The two newspapers published during the period, the *Londonderry Journal* and the *Ballyshannon Herald*, mainly ignored the hunger and fever epidemics that were devastating all of County Donegal, as if the famine were not really taking place at all.

It is amazing to read the reports from police, doctors, clergymen and other observers that were being sent to Dublin almost on a daily basis, and then to search these weekly newspapers and find no coverage of these subjects in the newspapers.

It is amazing that in any given week in 1847, when hundreds in Donegal would have died from hunger or disease, to find little attention paid to this ongoing tragedy, and to find no mention of the deaths.

It would appear that there was a deliberate conspiracy of silence, as if the editors had decided that their readers need not, or should not, be told of what was happening to the county or the country as a whole.

The result of this censorship was that the people living in Templecrone at the time had no idea that what was happening in their area was also happening in other areas, and, therefore, they did not know until long after the famine the extent of the tragedy.

However, this censorship had an impact long after the famine. Scholars in later years who were researching the impact of the famine in Donegal were first misled by the census data which masked the true extent of the death toll, and then when they turned to the contemporary newspapers and found little there, they had no reason to believe that the famine had any impact in Templecrone. The silence of later generations from Templecrone only helped confirm this erroneous idea.

The third reason that there is a lack of information on what happened at a local level stems from a reluctance by many Irish historians from the 1920s to the present, to confront the horror of the famine by getting into archives to study what really happened in local areas of Ireland.

The Great Hunger is often called the definitive study of the famine, and yet this work was written by an English woman and the approach was a broad sweep of the subject, not a close-up of any particular area.

The reasons why Irish historians shy away from the subject are complex. There is a reluctance to dwell on the gory details in any particular area, because this inevitably results in hostility to the British, and few historians want to stir up anti-British sentiment, in case this is confused with IRA-type republicanism.

Any in-depth examination of the record for local areas also reveals that the Irish people allowed themselves to be brutalized and reduced to the status of beggars, and it is very difficult for any scholar to accept the shame and humiliation graphically portrayed in the archives, because the Irish are inclined to view themselves as a warrior race who lost many wars but always fought back gamely, and there was little fighting back in Ireland during the famine just a timid acceptance of the extermination of their race.

So, those who have written about the famine in recent years are inclined to focus on the big picture and analyze the economics or the politics of the famine, and do not get down to the parish level and examine the brutal and horrible details.

And yet, it is the sum of all those horrors, which happened in every parish in Ireland, that adds up to the reality of what happened in Ireland during this period, and one cannot understand the whole famine experience unless one understands what happened at the local level.

* * *

CHAPTER NINETEEN
Northwest Donegal: After the Famine

According to an article which appeared in the *Times,* Northwest Donegal was on its way to recovery in July of 1850. Food seemed plentiful and rents once again were being paid on time. The correspondent noted that there was a lively commerce in hand-knitted woolen goods made in the Rosses, which were sold abroad and brought in much needed income to the women of the district. Kelp gathering was a huge commercial enterprise and it was being shipped to Scotland to be turned into iodine.

Perhaps the most notable indication that the people were gradually recovering was the appearance of poitin once again, a product that had vanished during famine years. No matter how much the Revenue Police tried to suppress the industry, it was being made in large batches out on the islands and out in the remote mountain glens for consumption by local people and for sale throughout Donegal.

The first sign of recovery among the small tenant farmers was not just a healthy potato and grain crop, but the appearance of a cow once again on the tiny family farm. The cows had begun to disappear in the summer of 46 when the potato crop failed for the second time, and by the end of Black 47 the livestock had all but disappeared from the Rosses.

Now, here and there, a tenant would proudly display a cow in a field near his home, as a sign to the world that this family had risen from the ashes of the famine.

But in spite of these outward signs of renewal, the reality of life in the Rosses and Gweedore was that the vast majority of the tenants were just one potato crop away from starvation, and that it would take a whole herd of cows or sheep to give some sense of security to these desperate people that a major failure of the potato crop would not bring a return of the horror years of the late forties.

One of the principle reasons that the tenants could never get very far back from the brink was the high rents which consumed most of the resources of these small tenants every year. Even though the women knitted, the men went to Scotland or the Lagan for seasonal work, and the whole family became involved in harvesting kelp, by the time the rent was paid there was little left over after the annual needs of the family were taken care of. It was an industrious and thrifty man, indeed, who had the resources to buy a cow, and this was why the presence of a cow on the farm after the famine was such a source of such family pride.

The resident landlords of the Rosses and Gweedore monitored the recovery of their tenants in 1848, 1849, and 1850, and after another bumper harvest in the summer of 1849, these landlords, which included Forster and Chorley in the Rosses, and Nixon, Hill, Olphert and Hamilton in Gweedore, got together and formed a plan to vastly increase their revenues. They planned to achieve this not only by increasing the rents but by asserting their absolute right to all of the resources on the estate, including unoccupied mountain lands, the harvesting of kelp, the harvesting of peat, and the control of all commerce on their estates, including the sale of woolen goods, and the operation of shops and bars.

They even asserted the right to all rocks and minerals one foot beneath the surface, and the rights to all fish and game that swam or walked on their estate or in the skies above it.

Obviously, these landlords saw their estates as profit centers and they believed that profits could be greatly increased if an entirely new way of doing business was introduced to the area. They believed that when they purchased these estates they became absolute masters of their property and that the tenants had an obligation to give in to whatever was demanded of them.

Some of these landlords had only recently acquired their holdings, like Hill in 1838, and the fact that the ancestors of the tenants had been in the area for a thousand years, was not a concern to the landlords, nor was the fact that the tenants believed that it was they who had the moral right to the land.

The decision of the landlords to assert their absolute ownership of the land, and to milk the last drop of revenue out of the tenants, set in motion a confrontation between the landlords and the tenants that dragged on for several generations. This conflict resulted in evictions, murders, sabotage, and media attention from around the world and partisan support for the tenants from such diverse individuals as prominent British aristocrats and ruthless Irish republicans.

The British police, army and navy eventually got involved in the struggle, and guns were smuggled in by the tenants. Both sides used the media expertly, and the landless masses of the Northwest used propaganda very effectively.

As time went on the goals of the tenants changed from tenants' rights in the early years of the struggle, to the economic destruction of the landlord system later on, and finally to winning control of their own farms by buying out the landlords.

The landlords won most of the skirmishes in the early years of the struggle, but as the struggle became nationwide, the British found it counterproductive to support the landlords and the landlords eventually went down to defeat.

Francis Forster fired the first shots of the war which was eventually to engulf the Northwest, when in November of 1849 he demanded that his tenants accept a rent increase that ranged from 100% to 200%, and to pay back arrears that had accrued from the famine years. The generous landlord who was a benefactor during the years of hunger had suddenly become the greedy tyrant who wanted to drain every asset from his tenants.

In addition, Forster decreed that from then onwards fees would be charged for the harvesting of seaweed for use as food or for fertilizer, and that other fees would be charged for harvesting peat. The mountain pastures, which the tenants had used for hundreds of years for common summer grazing would now be off limits to all except those who paid a fee.

Forster said those new terms would go into effect immediately, and those who did not pay would have their crops or livestock seized.

Forster had been a "good" landlord during the famine and had saved many lives, but now that this crisis was over, he was determined to become a rich man on the backs of those whose lives he had saved.

Forster was a magistrate and one of the smallest and least influential landowners in the area. He had no title, did not come from a family who was widely esteemed, and was in fact a local Protestant who had acquired holdings while acting as an agent.

But he had powerful landlord friends in neighboring estates, Lord Hill and the Rev Alex Nixon, and he was also part of a landlord/magistrate organization in Northwest Donegal which was determined to assert itself, and he knew that if the situation went into crisis, he could rely on his friends in Gweedore.

Forster's decision to act at this particular time was based on information that he had received that the tenants had formed a resistance movement, and that he had better act before it gained strength.

It is difficult to determine what reaction Forster expected from his tenants, but he could hardly have foreseen the sudden fury of the people, or the absolute determination they had not to pay the rent increases that was being demanded of them. Nor could he have foreseen how quickly they organized themselves to present him with a united front—a front that seemed determined to use all means, including violence, to obstruct his plans.

Most of Forsters's holdings were north of Dungloe in an area known as "the lower Rosses," and when Forster learned that among his tenants in Meenderranasloe, Annagry, was a tenant named Edward Rogers who was willing to pay the back rent but not the new rent, Forster decided that Rogers was a man he could deal with, because obviously Rogers was not a member of the organization lined up against him.

Rogers had one cow in his front garden, and Forster decided to move against Rogers.

On November 19, 1850, Forster sent four bailiffs, led by Fergil Boyle, to Meenderranasloe to seize the cow, and also to seize a cow from a Sweeney family, who were relatives of Rogers.

As the bailiffs approached the Rogers house they saw neighbors leave their homes and follow the bailiffs to the Rogers residence. The bailiffs testified later that hundreds of people began to gather on the high ground near the Rogers home, most of them carrying spade handles or clubs. Women and children were among the crowd, and they were armed with stones.

When the bailiffs came out of the Rogers house and moved towards the garden where the cow was tethered, his neighbors shouted at Rogers not to give up the cow, but he and his son Andy paid no attention to them and helped the bailiffs drive the cow, and another belonging to Michael Sweeney, across the mountain towards the pound in Dungloe, with the angry crowd in pursuit.

The crowd surrounded the bailiffs and Edward and Andy Rogers in a glen in the townland of Drimnacart and assaulted all six men with tree branches, spade handles and stones, giving Edward Rogers a fractured skull, and the four bailiffs multiple bruises and cuts.

Among those in the attacking party were Ned Sweeney, James Rogers, Paddy McCue, Bryan Duffy, Owen Boyle, James Cannon, Michael Farquar, and Sally Duffy. The cows were then driven away by the crowd, and the bailiffs were warned that if they ever came back to the area to seize cattle they would be killed, and that any tenant who gave up his cattle would get the same treatment.

One of the tenants told the bailiffs he would rather die fighting the landlord than give the landlord everything and then die of hunger.

The belligerence of the tenants was an indication that a sea change had taken place in their attitude since the famine. The horrors that they had endured during the famine left them with a determination to stand up for their rights and resist all attempts by the landlords to abuse them. The bailiffs beat a strategic retreat, and the tenants won the first skirmish of what was to be a long drawn out conflict.

The battle at Drimnacart is interesting for a number of reasons. First of all, it indicated that the tenants were well organized as early as the summer of 1849, and were using the same tactics that were used later a few miles away in Gweedore. This also became the classic methods of confrontation used 30 years later as reflected in the Plan of Campaign and the Boycott strategies of the Land League.

Secondly, the tenants were willing to battle the landlord openly, knowing well that the bailiffs would identify them and turn their names into the landlord and the police. Prior to that there had been acts of sabotage committed by masked men at night, activities attributed to the Ribbonmem and those involved in this type of activity went to great lengths to conceal their identity.

The Drimnacart battle was more like an insurrection than a rent dispute, and in the years ahead there would be a number of such battles.

In a way it was the first skirmish in Donegal of a new war against British interests in Ireland. The Famine had clearly demonstrated to the tenants that the English and their representatives in Ireland had no hesitation in enforcing policies that could have fatal consequences for Irish people, and these small tenants had decided that they had two choices: they either fight for the lives of their families, or emigrate with their families abroad. Those who decided to stay in Northwest Donegal decided to fight.

Forster responded in a number of ways and one can only assume that his response was carefully planned in advance.

First, he brought the bailiffs over to Bunbeg, Gweedore, and had them testify to the attacks to an assembly of magistrates, who were also the major hardline landlords in the area. Forster also made a statement that the bailiffs were only collecting rents lawfully imposed, and that they were attacked while doing their duty.

Then he petitioned the Lord Lieutenant in Dublin Castle, asking for fifteen additional police to be assigned to him because his life and property were being threatened. The Lord Lieutenant sent the police into the Rosses to assist Forster.

These armed police were then used to support the bailiffs and seize cattle, or if there was no cattle on the farm to seize the potato crop or anything else of value that could be seized.

None of the tenants gave anything willingly, but gradually Forster got his pound of flesh, with the help of a small army of bailiffs, police, and revenue police. The revenue police were Customs officials who were cracking down on poitin making, and on smuggling, both favorite activities along the coast.

Forster did not evict anyone during this period, and he refrained from this because he knew that he would never get a tenant to replace an evicted tenant. A tenant who took the holding of an evicted tenant would risk an attack by local vigilantes.

There is no record of any convictions of those who participated in the Drumnacart incident either. Perhaps Forster did not want to get involved in legal proceedings that would only make heroes of the rebels and make the situation much worse, and so he left them alone.

As Forster's army went around the area seizing property and threatening the lives of those tenants who tried to resist, James MacBride, a community leader from Bunbeg, Gweedore, sent a memorial to the Lord Lieutenant on behalf of the Rosses tenants complaining of the activities of Forster and demanded that the fifteen additional police be withdrawn.

MacBride argued that Forster's statement that he was afraid for his life and his property was ridiculous that it was the lives of the tenants that were being threatened and it was their property that was under siege. MacBride compared Forster to a highwayman who was robbing the people of their basic necessities.

But the Lord Lieutenant wrote a curt one paragraph letter dismissing MacBride's request that the police be withdrawn. The Lord Lieutenant did not acknowledge tenant grievances either.

But he would have been wise to pay more attention to a population that was organizing a resistance movement that obviously did not rule out violence. Such movements had led to widespread violence in the past.

Eighteen months after the Drimnacart battle, in May of 1852, the British Coastguard swarmed into Inishman Island off the Gweedore coast and turned all the houses on the island inside out looking for guns and poitin-making equipment.

The revenue police put on a massive display of force, stationing gunboats around the island to make sure nobody escaped, and landing swarms of police in full battle gear on the island to make sure they could handle any armed resistance. But they did not find guns nor did they find any distilling equipment.

The raid had been staged in the first place because the British had been supplied with information by Father Doherty, a Gweedore priest, that arms had been smuggled into Inishman by the islanders. The islanders had heard that the Coastguard was going to raid the island and confiscate their poitin equipment and jail anyone they found in possession of poitin. The islanders were determined to go to war over the issue.

This was another demonstration of a post famine change in the behavior of the tenants of Northwest Donegal, who were no longer willing to accept abuse from British authorities.

Father Doherty said he told the Coastguard of the plan because he was afraid there would be a bloodbath, with heavy casualties on both sides, and then he told the islanders that the Coastguard was aware of their plans and they should not resist an invasion. So, the islanders hid the arms and the equipment on the mainland, and the revenue police found nothing when they arrived.

The British authorities tried to force Father Doherty to reveal the names of those involved in the gunrunning, but he refused and the issue was not pressed.

The Inishman invasion was followed by a report that tenants on the Nixon estate in Gweedore were also importing guns and were prepared to do battle with Nixon and his bailiffs over outrageous rents, evictions, and the fencing in of traditional grazing grounds. This belligerence was also the result of the fury that was a result of the famine experience.

The Reverend Alexander Nixon was a Protestant clergyman who lived in Cloich Cheann Fhaola and who devoted far more time to squeezing the last penny out of his tenants than he spent at preaching the gospel. He was in fact a landlord who just happened to be a clergyman, and the managing of his estate was his major activity.

In the summer of 1852 it was obvious that all the landlords in the Gweedore area had formed a union, because all of them began to raise rents and put restrictions on various activities, like mountain grazing, kelp harvesting, and the harvesting of peat, activities that the tenants had engaged in freely up to this point without any additional fees.

And it was equally obvious that the landlords were prepared to do battle over these issues, just as the tenants were determined to establish that they had the right to occupy the land their ancestors had lived on for a thousand years.

While the landlords drew up their battle plans, the Gweedore tenants also drew up their plan of campaign, and they found an able new leader in Father John Doherty, who had recently been assigned to Gweedore.

Doherty took over complete control of the tenant organization and one of the first things he did was to prevent the Inishman islanders from going into mortal combat with the British armed forces. He told them that those who were not killed in battle would die on the gallows.

Doherty replaced Father Hugh McFadden who had been a tireless worker for his people during the famine and who complained frequently to Dublin Castle about the conduct of the landlords.

The two men had very different temperaments, however. McFadden was a spokesman for his people and he solicited food to keep them alive, but he was not a revolutionary.

Doherty on the other hand was willing to go much further, and while the evidence was not there to convict him for being involved in acts of sabotage and violent civil disobedience, there was no doubt he knew who the more violent of his parishioners were and who was involved in each violent retaliation against a landlord.

Father Doherty was born near Glenties and he had witnessed the horrors of the famine first hand, especially on the Conyngham Estate where the tenants were given no help by the landlord.

He had also witnessed the swarms of destitute people from the Rosses and Lettermacaward swarm around the Glenties Poorhouse begging for admission, only to be denied admission because of overcrowding and allowed to die in the streets outside. And he had been inside the Poorhouse and saw the dead and the living lying together on beds of putrid straw... and these were scenes he would never forget.

When he became a priest he was determined to work for the welfare of his people both physical and spiritual, and the most traumatic aspect of the famine for him was that he was not able to save the lives of those he had sworn to serve. In the aftermath of the famine he became their champion, leading them into battle and speaking out on their behalf when they were unable to speak for themselves.

Perhaps the one single act that best illustrated the dedication of Doherty came in the winter of 1854 when a poor harvest left many of the Gweedore parishioners close to starvation.

Doherty first asked the Lord Lieutenant for emergency food supplies, but when the government turned him down, he went to a merchant named Moffatt in Dunfanaghy and got 1,500 pounds sterling worth of Indian meal on credit about 150,000 pounds sterling at today's rate of exchange and distributed the meal to his people. He had all the money paid back within eighteen months.

When Doherty took control of the tenant leadership in Gweedore he used the same tactics that the Rosses tenants had used against Forster, but he made them much more effective by not only enforcing penalties against erring landlords, but imposing penalties against those tenants who did not follow all of his commands.

During the next two years, Doherty organized boycotts of the grazing areas that the landlords were now charging tenant's fees for their use, and organizing protests all over the county over the way the Gweedore tenants were being treated. And according to the Reverend Nixon he was intimidating Catholic bailiffs by refusing to hear their confessions if they followed the landlord's orders, and he even introduced an array of fines which he imposed on tenants who did not follow orders.

The landlords complained to Bishop Patrick McGettigan about Doherty's activities and Doherty was reprimanded, but this achieved nothing and the stakes were raised on both sides, as bailiffs were assaulted and landlord property attacked, and the landlords dug in and continued to raise rents and impose other fees on the beleaguered tenants.

Finally, the landlords introduced a more dangerous element into this volatile mix, when Hill and some of the other landlords announced that they were going to lease vast stretches of the mountain areas to Scots and English sheep farmers, and these sheep farmers in turn were going to import thousands of blackface sheep into the area and graze them where the tenants had traditionally grazed their flocks.

To make matters worse, some of the landlords indicated a desire to build new Protestant churches, and bring in "new blood" into the area to fill up the chapels of these churches, but this effort failed, as did most of the other designs of the landlords.

At the time, it seemed to Doherty and his flock that the landlords intended to drive all the Catholic Irish off the land and replace them with loyalists from Scotland and England. It was seen as a new phase of the Plantation of Ulster.

The hostilities escalated in December of 1856 into what became known in Donegal history as "The Sheep War" a war that was to attract a great deal of publicity all over the British Isles, until it ended in mid-1858. Before it was over whole armies of police were brought into Gweedore to control the tenants.

The first shot was fired in the Sheep War in December of 1856 when forty young men raided the house of James Lillco, one of the new Scottish sheep farmers who had settled on a remote area named Altan, and told him to get out of Ireland if he valued his life. All forty were well dressed all in white shirts and Lillco said later that they must have been from outside the area as he did not recognize any of them.

The raid on Altan was followed by raids on the houses of other shepherds in the mountains and this was followed by the disappearance of hundreds of blackface sheep, many of whom were found dead. Doherty was believed to be orchestrating the guerrilla warfare and to be supervising the logistics involved in each incident.

By the following March more than 600 sheep had been lost, and pedigree rams had been castrated, and James Wright, one of the first sheep farmers to arrive, sold out his remaining stock and went back to Scotland.

The authorities fought back on two fronts in an attempt to defeat the insurgents. First they got a grand jury comprised of landlords to levy a tax known as the Sheep Tax on all the householders in Gweedore to pay for the missing or dead sheep, thus making all the citizens of Gweedore pay for the actions of those who were waging war.

Next, scores of additional police were brought into the area to patrol the mountains and new barracks were built in several areas in the parish, and then a further tax called the Police Tax was levied to pay for this additional security.

The behavior of the British Administration in Ireland showed that the government was totally behind the landlords, even when the landlords were behaving in a manner which was being widely condemned all over the British Isles.

The reaction of the tenants was the destruction of a barracks built at Tor and the destruction of a shepherd's house in the same area, which was followed by the disappearance of hundreds more sheep.

Doherty next took the battle to a new level by sending a petition with 2,027 signatures to the House of Commons, urging parliament to intervene in the dispute. This action received a great deal of publicity and soon the Sheep War was in the media all over the British Isles. But Parliament rejected the petition on the grounds that only three of the signatures were genuine.

Daniel Cruise, a resident magistrate, then met with three leaders of the Irish Catholic Hierarchy in early June, and he told Joseph Dixon, archbishop of Armagh and primate of All Ireland; Paul Cullen, archbishop of Dublin; and Doherty's bishop, Patrick McGettigan, that Doherty was a dangerous troublemaker and he should be removed from Gweedore. The bishops agreed with him, and Bishop McGettigan went to Gweedore and berated Doherty in front of a crowd assembled outside the chapel in Derrybeg.

He then castigated the parishioners for defying the British:

"England has sent out an army to the Crimea, and she has conquered the Russians; she has now sent an army to China, and she has conquered the Chinese; and do you mean to tell me that you, a small corner of a parish in the county Donegal, mean to stand up and say you will oppose the law of England?"

But this was exactly what the people of Gweedore had in mind, and the bishop's criticism notwithstanding, the parishioners continued with the war even though Doherty was immediately transferred out of the area in September and was replaced by Father Daniel McGee, a historian who had no taste for making history.

The attempt by the authorities to collect the police and sheep taxes was hampered by the unwillingness of the tax collectors to demand the tax. Hugh McBride of Bunbeg, a tax collector, refused to collect the tax and was fired, joining his brother James among the unemployed. James had already been fired by Hill for releasing seized cattle from the pound, and he had also been labeled a troublemaker by the landlords for his authorship of a memorial to the Lord Lieutenant over the plight of the Forster tenants in the Rosses.

The McBrides were descendants of a leading Gaelic family who had refused to compromise with the English after the defeat of the Gaelic chieftains in the early 17th century, and their heritage showed in their stand against the landlords in the middle of the 19th century. In an era when jobs were almost nonexistent they sacrificed their jobs for the cause, and in an era when it could be very dangerous to defy the British, they stood up and were counted, and were willing to pay the price, whatever the price was.

But Magistrate Cruise was determined to collect the taxes anyway, and when he could not induce any local person to act as a tax collector he appointed Head Constable William Young as collector, and Young accompanied by up to 30 constables marched from house to house terrorizing old people and frightening many younger tenants into to give up their last penny. The whole spectacle brought no honor to either the police or the landlords.

The intimidation of the tenants became even more acute when a William McGarvey, in Lifford Jail for poaching, gave information about those involved in sheep stealing, and as a result of this a number of the most prominent leaders in the parish were arrested, including James McBride, who was accused of being the ringleader.

After the arrest of McBride and the others, and the departure of Doherty, resistance collapsed among some of the tenants, and a few of those who could pay the taxes paid them.

But the affair was far from over. A number of prominent Irish newspapers, including the *Nation*, the *Londonderry Standard*, and the *Ulsterman*, continued to support the campaign, and a historian named Holland, a nationalist who had a venomous attitude towards landlords, kept up a continuous barrage of support for the tenants.

Holland accused the sheep farmers of inflating the number of sheep stolen in order to gain financially, and accused them of outright theft when he stated that they had sold sheep which they had claimed were lost. Holland's investigation also revealed that the sheep farmers had been selling excessive amounts of wool they could not have had if the sheep were missing.

Holland also pointed out that the shepherds were claiming 17 shillings for each dead sheep, while the live sheep were only worth 10 shillings thus they had an incentive to kill the sheep, earn the higher price, and then sell the wool. And the worst aspect of all this, according to Holland, was that the poor Irish farmers were being made foot the bill for the criminal activities of these foreigners.

Other newspapers took up the hue and cry about the persecuted tenants of Gweedore and collections were made all over Ireland and Britain to relieve the extreme distress. Father Doherty orchestrated much of the publicity even though he was no longer in the parish, and he persuaded a dozen priests to join him in his work.

Protestants who disliked landlords were also involved in the struggle, especially Presbyterians, who were active in fund raising and disseminating anti-landlord information all over Ulster.

But the relentless pressure being put on the tenants by the constabulary who continuously harassed them, led to a final surrender of the tenants by 1859, and the sheep stealing tapered off, and no matter how much support the tenants were getting from the outside, ultimately they were alone when they faced the power of the landlord and many just did not have the endurance to continue.

A few desperate tenants tried to murder Alex Nixon, but when that attempt failed, the tenants retreated into a bitter silence. The Sheep War was over.

* * *

Although the landlords would claim victory in 1860 in their war with the tenants in Gweedore, it was very clear that they had not won a great deal. The last Scots sheep farmer departed after the tenants were beaten into submission, so the plan to bring outside planters unraveled, and the landlords had reaped such a hurricane of bad publicity over their treatment of their tenants that some of them came to the conclusion that the war had gained them little, or nothing.

Between 1860 and 1864 life in Gweedore and elsewhere in the Northwest was marked by an apathy among the tenants, and an increase in immigration to Australia and the United States. The inhabitants of Gweedore had been left without a leader with the departure of Father Doherty and the prison sentences imposed on other community leaders.

However, elsewhere in Ireland there was a growing movement to reform the whole landlord system of land ownership in order to make it possible for small farmers to own their leased holdings. At the core of this movement was the belief that the small farmers of Ireland would never have an incentive to improve their holdings until they held title to the property.

As this movement grew in strength, a new leader appeared on the Gweedore scene—a priest named Father James McFadden, who would become just as controversial as Father John Doherty or Father Hugh McFadden.

Father James McFadden toured the parish after his arrival and urged all the tenants to present a united front to the landlord. In the following years he organized rent strikes, boycotts, and in 1882 he founded a branch of the National Land League in Gweedore.

George Hill died in 1879 and the estate passed to his son, Captain Arthur Hill. Captain Hill appointed a relative, Somerset Ward as bailiff, and Ward began a brutal campaign against tenants who were behind in their rents, including widows who had no income to pay the rent.

McFadden reacted by organizing a boycott of Hill's stores, and by prohibiting any parishioner to work in the hotel, or to knit woolen goods for Hill's export business. In 1888 Hill had McFadden arrested and sentenced to six months in prison for his activities, and he was prohibited from organizing any more boycotts or rent strikes.

But in 1889, McFadden was again organizing strikes, this time in the Olphert estate, which was adjacent to the Hill estate, and a warrant was issued for his arrest. When a group of police arrived at the parish house led by Detective Inspector Martin to arrest McFadden, they were stoned by parishioners and Martin died from injuries inflicted on him. This was the bloody climax to the 40-year war between landlords and tenants in Northwest Donegal. McFadden and a dozen parishioners were charged with murder, but the charges against McFadden were dropped, and the other defendants served prison sentences.

In the aftermath of the Martin murder, open confrontations between landlords and tenants ceased, but the battle was resumed in the courts, and gradually the landlords were forced to reduce rents and return the mountain grazing areas to the tenants. The landlord's stranglehold on commerce in the Northwest was also abolished and businessmen from the ranks of the Catholic majority emerged to become the major business leaders in the area. Eventually the vast estates were broken up and the tenants were allowed to purchase their holdings.

The role of the three activist priests in the Gweedore tenant-landlord struggle receives little attention from historians, and even today a great number of the present–day inhabitants of Gweedore are not aware that there were two Father McFaddens involved in the struggle.

Father John Doherty gets less attention, even though he was a breed of activist who was almost a revolutionary and he was a community leader in Northwest Donegal who always fought openly for civil rights and could not be intimidated by the establishment.

There are two questions posed by the tenant wars in Northwest Donegal that deserve some attention. The first question is why was it that it was the clergymen in the area who played a leading role in the fight for tenant rights, and not the descendants of the old Gaelic aristocracy? The answer to that question is that priests could get away with a lot more than private citizens, because the establishment was afraid to crack down on priests because it might provoke a far more serious confrontation, like the Inspector Martin murder.

The second question is why the goal of the priests was the reform of the landlord system, and not the creation of an independent nation, free of English domination. The answer to that question is that the Church approved a limited degree of social reform, but was terrified of revolution. Revolution in France and other European countries had often led to attacks on the influence of the Catholic Church, and that was to be avoided at all costs. This is why the bishops pulled Father John Doherty out of Gweedore: he was seen as a dangerous revolutionary.

But revolution came anyway, even after the British cracked down on the landlords and recognized the rights of tenants. A process of total alienation from England that began with the horror of the famine and continued for the rest of the 19th century and led to the Rebellion of 1916.

Ireland had decided it was time to break the link with England and manage its own destiny, and the roots of the insurrection was in the British treatment of the Irish in the famine of the 1840s.

NOTES

Chapter One

1. James H. Tuke, *Report to the Society of Friends*, p. 147.
2. W.C. Forster, *Report to the Society of Friends*.
3. *The Census of Ireland for the Year 1841; 1851.*

Chapter Two

1. George Nicholls, *Report on Poor Laws in Ireland*, 1835.
2. John O'Donovan, *Letters From Donegal*, 1835.

Chapter Three

1. *The Census of Ireland for the Year 1841.*
2. John O'Donovan, *Letters from Donegal*, 1835.

   Thomas Campbell Foster, *The Times*, London, September 1, 1845.

   Donnchadh Devenney, *Footprints through the Rosses*.

Chapter Four

1. Thomas Campbell Foster, *The Times*, London, September 1, 1845.
2. *Burke's Landed Gentry.*
3. *The Great Castles of Ireland.*
4. *Burke's Landed Gentry.*
5. Thomas Campbell Foster, *The Times*, London, September 1, 1845.

6. *The Times*, October 16, 1845.

7. *The Times*, October 22, 1845.

Chapter Five

1. Cecil Woodham Smith, *The Great Hunger*.

2. Ibid.

3. Canon John O'Rourke, *The Great Irish Famine*.

4. *The Londonderry Journal*, October 17.

5. *The Londonderry Journal*, October 8.

6. *The Londonderry Journal*, October 8.

7. The Irish Folklore Commission Archives, *Famine Notebooks, Northwest Donegal*, University College Dublin.

8. *Distress Papers (1846)*, D85W, Templecrone.

Chapter Six

1. *Peel Memoirs, Vol. 11*.

2. Cecil Woodham Smith, *The Great Hunger*.

3. *Famine Relief Papers*, Donegal, Templecrone, Foster to Stewart II/3.

Chapter Seven

1. *Distress Papers (1846)*, D85W, Templecrone, D/836, 3/27/46.

2. *Griffith Valuations, 1857*.

3. *Distress Papers (1846), Templecrone, 1441*. Cornelius Ward to Capt. Kennedy.

4. *Trevelyn Memorandum on Board of Works*, July 22, 1846, 766/364.

5. Lord Brougham, House of Lords, March 23, Hansard, Vol. 84, pp. 139-67.

6. The Irish Folklore Commission Archives, *Famine Notebooks*, Northwest Donegal, University College Dublin.

7. Ibid.

8. Ibid.

9. *Outrage Reports, Donegal, 1846* (1512), April, T/8631.

10. *The Londonderry Journal,* April 8, 1846, Letter from Mullaghderg Committee.

11. *The Londonderry Journal*, April 15, 1846, Unsigned Letter.

12. *The Londonderry Journal*, April 29, 1846, Unsigned Letter.

13. *The Londonderry Journal*, May 20, 1846, Unsigned Letter.

14. Ibid.

15. *Famine Relief Papers* (1846), iv/2.

16. *The Londonderry Journal,* June 17, 1846, Advertisement.

Chapter Eight

1. Cecil Woodham Smith, *The Great Hunger,* Chapter 6.

2. Ibid.

3. Canon John O'Rourke, *The Great Irish Famine,* Chapter 5.

4. Ibid.

5. *The Londonderry Journal,* September 9, 1846.

6. *Famine Relief Papers,* Donegal, 1846, T.L. Molloy to Relief Commissioner, Dublin Castle, August 3, 1846.

7. *Famine Relief Papers* (1846), ii/ 1, 5598, Donegal, Valentine Griffith to William Stanley.

8. *The Londonderry Journal,* Friday, September 4, 1846.

10. The Irish Folklore Commission Archives, *Famine Notebooks,* Donegal, University College Dublin

11. *Arranmore Links.*

12. Mrs. Dessie Sweeney, Sweeney's Hotel Dungloe, Interview, 1993.

13. Ibid.

14. The Irish Folklore Commission Archives, *Famine Notebooks,* Donegal, University College Dublin.

15. *Famine Relief Papers*

16. *Famine Relief Papers* (1847), Donegal, Public Appeal by Lord George Hill, January 11, 1847.

17. *Famine Relief Papers* (1847), #9174, Griffith to Routh, January 12, 1847.

Chapter Nine

1. *Famine Relief Papers,* #9826.

2. *The Londonderry Journal,* October 10, 1846.

3. *Famine Relief Papers* (1846), Donegal, #6636, 06152, Griffith to Routh, October 26, 1846.

4. *Famine Relief Papers* (1846), Donegal, #6825, Griffith to Routh, October 28, 1846.

5. *Famine Relief Papers* (1846), Donegal, 06713, McFadden to Routh, October 27, 1846.

6. *Famine Relief Papers* (1846), Donegal, #5797.

7. *Famine Relief Papers* (1846), Forster to Routh, November 6, 1846.

8. James H. Tuke's, *Report to the Society of Friends,* December 1846.

9. *The Londonderry Journal*, January 6, 1847.

10. Society of Friends, *Transactions of the Central Relief Committee,* Appendix XI.

11. *Outrage Reports,* Donegal, January 1847, 46.434M.

12. *Famine Relief Papers* (1847), Donegal, #9825, #9826, Forster to Routh.

13. Sir William P. MacArthur, *Medical History of the Famine,*

14. Cecil Woodham Smith, *The Great Hunger*, Chapter 9.

15. *Famine Relief Papers* (1847), Belfast Ladies Association Report, #9825.

Chapter Ten

1. Cecil Woodham Smith, *The Great Hunger*, Chapter 9.

2. Ibid.

3. Ibid, Appendix III.

4. *Final Report to the Society of Friends.*

5. George Hancock's *Letters to the Society of Friends*, February 23, 1847.

    William Bennett's *Report to the Society of Friends*, Dungloe, March 23, 1847.

6. *The Londonderry Journal*, March 10, 1847.

7. *Famine Relief Papers* (1847), Donegal, #14620, Molloy to Routh.

8. Ibid.

9. *The Londonderry Journal, January 20, 1847, Page I.*

10. *The Londonderry Journal*, April 21, 1847.

11. *The Londonderry Journal*, April 14, 1847.

Chapter Eleven

1. *Irish Folklore Commission Archives, Famine Notebooks, Donegal, University College Dublin.*

2. Ibid.

3. *Relief of Distress Papers, Quakers, 2/505/25, Ulster Subcommittee Record Book, Francis Forster.*

4. *Famine Relief Papers (1847), Donegal, 15.716, Molloy to Relief Commission, March 24, 1847.*

5. *Outrage Reports (1847), Donegal, 302/24, Lame Reports, June 16, 1847.*

6. *The Londonderry Journal*, May 20, 1847.

Chapter Twelve

1. Lord John Russell to Clarendon, 21, 1847, *Clarendon Papers*, I A.

2. Cecil Woodham Smith, *The Great Hunger*, Chapter 15.

3. *Outrage Reports*, Donegal (1847), Forster to Under Secretary Dublin Castle, September 17, 1847.

4. Anseth Nicholson, *Lights and Shades of Ireland* (1850), pp. 259-277.

5. *Letters of Richard D. Webb* to Central Relief Committee Society of Friends, Distress in Erris, May 5, 1847.

6. *Dublin Evening Mail*, November 5, I 847.

7. Denis Holland, *The Landlords in Donegal.*

8. Arranmore Links.

9. *British Parliamentary Papers, Irish Famine Series*, Sixth Series (Vol. 56), pp. *344354.*

10. *Arranmore Links.*

11. Denis Holland, T*he Landlords in Donegal.*

Chapter Thirteen

1. *British Parliamentary Papers, Irish Famine Series*, Sixth Series (Vol. 50) pp. 351.

2. The Irish Folklore Commission Archives, *Famine Notebooks,* Donegal, University College Dublin.

3. *British Parliamentary Papers, Irish Famine Series,* Sixth Series (Vol. 56) pp. 64.

4. *British Parliamentary Papers, Irish Famine Series*, Sixth Series (Vol. 56) pp. 347.

5. Cecil Woodham Smith, *The Great Hunger*, Chapter 16.

6. Abbe James MacGeoghegan, *The History of Ireland,* Chapter by J. Mitchel.

Chapter Fourteen

1. Cecil Woodham Smith, *The Great Hunger*, Chapter 17.

2. *Final Report of Relief Commission,* Appendix XXIV, Trevelyn to Pim; Pim to Trevelyn, June 1849.

3. Cecil Woodham Smith, *The Great Hunger*, Chapter 18.

Chapter Fifteen

1. *The Londonderry Journal*, January 30, 1850, Reprint of *Times* article.
2. The Irish Folklore Commission Archives, *Famine Notebooks,* Donegal, University College Dublin.
3. Mrs. Dessie Sweeney, Dungloe, Co. Donegal, Interview.

Chapter Sixteen

1. *The Census of Ireland for the Year 1841.*
2. Abbe James MacGeoghegan, *The History of Ireland,* Chapter by J. Mitchel.
3. Thomas Campbell Foster, *The Times,* September 1, 1845.

BIBLIOGRAPHY

Bateman, John. *The Great Landowners of Great Britain and Ireland.*

Butt, Isaac. *A Voice for Ireland, The Famine in the Land,* 1857.

Carlisle, Nicholas. *A Topographical Dictionary of Ireland,* 1810.

Coleman, Terry. *Going to America.*

Conyngham, David P. *Ireland, Past and Present.*

Coote, Charles *History of the Union.*

The Cope, Diamond Jubilee, 1906, 1981.

Cousens, S.H. *The Regional Variation in Mortality During the Great Irish Famine*

Curtis, E. *History of Ireland.*

Devenney, Donnchadh. *Footprints Through the Rosses.*

Doherty, Jenny and Doherty, Liz. *That Land Beyond: Folklore of Donegal.*

Donegal Annual

Edwards, R. Dudley and Desmond, T. Editors, *The Great Famine.*

Foster, Thomas Campbell. *Letters on the Condition of the People of Ireland, 1846.*

Freeman, W.T. *PreFamine Ireland.*

Gallagher, Barney. *Arranmore Links,* 1986.

Gallagher, Thomas. *Paddy's Lament.*

Gash, Norman. *Sir Robert Peel.*

Griffiths, A.R.G. *The Irish Board of Works in the Famine Years.*

Hill, Lord George. *Facts from Gweedore.*

Holland, Denis. *The Landlords in Donegal.*

Irish University Press, *Famine Series.*

Johnson, Clifton. *Life in the Irish Bogland*, 1901.

Kee, R. *Ireland: A History.*

Keegan, Gerald. *Famine Diary.*

Lawson, John Parker. *The Gazetteer of Ireland*, 1842.

MacManus, Seamus. *The Donegal Wonder Book*, 1826.

MacParlan, James. *Statistical Survey of the County of Donegal.*

Mitchel, John. *The Last Conquest of Ireland.*

Mokyr, J. *Why Ireland Starved.*

Nicholls, Sir George. *A History of the Irish Poor Law*, 1856.

Nicholson, Anseth. *Lights and Shades of Ireland*, 1850.

O'Gallagher, Marianna. Grosse Ile.

O'Gallchobhair, Proinnsias. *History of Landlordism in Donegal,* 1962.

O'Grada, Cormac. *The Great Irish Famine.*

O'Rourke, *History of the Great Irish Famine,* 1875.

Salaman, *History and Social Influence of the Potato.*

Sharkey, Olive. *Old Days, Old Ways.*

Tuathaigh, Gearoid O. *Ireland Before the Famine 1798 – 1848.*

Smith, Cecil Woodham. *The Great Hunger.*

Transactions of the Central Relief Committee of the Society of Friends During the Famine in Ireland 1846 and 1847.

Trench, William Steurt. *Realities of Irish Life,* 1869.

Tuke, James Hack. *A Visit to Connaught in the Autumn of 1847.*

Walpole, *Lord John Russell*.

Wigham, Maurice J. *The Irish Quakers*.

House built for the Conynghams in Burtonport (center). The 2nd Marquis stayed there on only one occasion during his lifetime.

Lackbeg House. Residence of Conyngham's agents.

Sweeney's Hotel Dungloe. In business since 1750.

The Bridge Inn, Dungloe. It was known as Campbell's Hotel during the period 1920-1965. It was known as Hanlon's Temperance Hotel during the famine.

Ruins of Conyngham warehouse in Burtonport.
Used as fever hospital during famine.

Conyngham's Grain Mill, Dungloe.

Roman Catholic Church, Dungloe. It had a thatch roof during the famine.

Church of Ireland Chapel (Protestant), Dungloe.

The Rectory, Maghery. Residence of the Reverend Valentine Pole Griffith.

Huge stone walls built by the Reverend Valentine Pole Griffith during the famine. Walls served no purpose other than to provide work for destitute people in Maghery area.

A Molly Maguire Story

By Patrick Campbell

On June 21, 1877, 10 Irish Americans were executed in the mining areas of Pennsylvania. All were accused of being members of a terrorist group called the Molly Maguires, and all were convicted of planning and carrying out the murder of a number of mining officials. Ten more Irish Americans were executed in Pennsylvania in the next 18 months on the same charges. One of the men executed on June 21, 1877, was Alexander Campbell, grand-uncle of the author.

The Molly Maguire executions generated a great deal of controversy in Pennsylvania from the 1870s to the present, with Irish Americans claiming the Mollies were framed by the mine owners, while other ethnic groups believe that they were guilty as charged and deserved the punishment they received.

The author first heard about the execution of his granduncle back in the late 1940s in Dungloe, County Donegal, Ireland, and in the early 1970s, while living in New Jersey, began a fifteen- year investigation into the entire Molly Maguire controversy in order to determine if Alexander Campbell was guilty or innocent.

A Molly Maguire Story is an account of that investigation.

"A frightening tale of a perverted legal system" *The Irish Echo.* New York, NY

"A dark page in Irish-American history" Celtic News Service. Illinois

"An eye-opening expose" *The Jersey Journal.* Jersey City, NJ

"An eye-opener" *Citizens' Voice.* Wilkes-Barre, PA

Published by

P.H. Campbell

82 Bentley Avenue Jersey City, NJ 07304 (201) 434-2432

ISBN 978-1505995589

Made in the USA
Middletown, DE
13 July 2023

35030541R00109